AAT

D1581289

DEVOLVED ASSESSMENT KIT

Foundation Unit 1

Recording Income and Receipts

August 2000 edition

This new Devolved Assessment Kit for Unit 1 *Recording Income and Receipts* follows the revised Foundation Standards of Competence. It contains:

- The **revised standards in full**, including guidance from the AAT on **evidence requirements, sources of evidence and assessment strategy**

- **Practice Devolved Assessments**

- **Trial Run Devolved Assessments**

FOR 2000 AND 2001 DEVOLVED ASSESSMENTS

BPP Publishing
August 2000

First edition August 2000

ISBN 0 7517 6203 X

British Library Cataloguing-in-Publication Data
A catalogue record for this book
is available from the British Library

Published by

BPP Publishing Limited
Aldine House, Aldine Place
London W12 8AW

www.bpp.com

Printed in Great Britain by W M Print
45 –47 Frederick Street
Walsall
West Midlands WS2 9NE

We are grateful to the Lead Body for Accounting for permission to reproduce extracts from the Standards of Competence for Accounting.

INTRODUCTION (iv)

How to use this Devolved Assessment Kit - Unit 1 Standards of Competence - Assessment Strategy

ORDER FORM

REVIEW FORM & FREE PRIZE DRAW

BPP PUBLISHING

HOW TO USE THIS DEVOLVED ASSESSMENT KIT

Aims of this Devolved Assessment Kit

> To help you succeed in the devolved assessment for Foundation Unit 1 *Recording Income and Receipts*.

To pass the devolved assessment you need a thorough understanding in all areas covered by the standards of competence. Devolved assessment may be in the workplace, although it is more likely to take the form of simulation. Either way, you need practical experience of relevant tasks.

> To tie in with the other components of the BPP Effective Study Package to ensure you have the best possible chance of success.

Interactive Text
This covers all you need to know for the devolved assessment for Unit 1 *Recording Income and Receipts*. Icons clearly mark key areas of the text. Numerous activities throughout the text help you practise what you have just learnt.

Devolved Assessment Kit
When you have understood and practised the material in the Interactive Text, you will have the knowledge and experience to tackle the Devolved Assessment Kit for Unit 1 *Recording Income and Receipts*. This aims to get you through the devolved assessment, whether in the form of the AAT simulation or in the workplace.

Recommended approach to this Devolved Assessment Kit

(a) Work through the **practice devolved assessments** first. These are meant to test specific performance criteria in depth to make sure you really understand them. They concentrate on particular areas rather than testing everything.

(b) Do the **trial run devolved assessments**. These aim to be similar to the AAT's own simulations, so you'll know what you'll be up against. Remember - devolved assessments are not time pressured, but a high level of accuracy is required.

(c) If your devolved assessment is in the **workplace** you should still do the trial run papers. These are based on practical, 'real life' situations, and the more practice you can get the better!

This approach is only a suggestion. Your college may well adapt it to suit your needs.

Remember this is a **practical** course.

(a) Try to relate the material to your experience in the workplace or any other work experience you may have had.

(b) Try to make as many links as you can to your study of the other Units at Foundation level.

(c) Keep this kit, (hopefully) you will find it invaluable in your everyday work too!

BPP Note: AAT Sample Devolved Assessment

At the time this Devolved Assessment Kit went to print (August 2000), sample devolved assessment simulations were not available. However, the Assessment Tasks in this Kit cover all performance criteria and are representative of the kind of tasks you may face.

UNIT 1 STANDARDS OF COMPETENCE

The structure of the Standards for Unit 1

The Unit commences with a statement of the **knowledge and understanding** which underpin competence in the Unit's elements.

The Unit of Competence is then divided into **elements of competence** describing activities which the individual should be able to perform.

Each element includes:

(a)   **A** set of **performance criteria.** This defines what constitutes competent performance.

(b)   A **range statement.** This defines the situations, contexts, methods etc in which competence should be displayed.

(c)   **Evidence requirements.** These state that competence must be demonstrated consistently, over an appropriate time scale with evidence of performance being provided from the appropriate sources.

(d)   **Sources of evidence.** These are suggestions of ways in which you can find evidence to demonstrate that competence. These fall under the headings: 'observed performance; work produced by the candidate; authenticated testimonies from relevant witnesses; personal account of competence; other sources of evidence.'

The elements of competence for Unit 1 *Recording Income and Receipts* are set out below. Knowledge and understanding required for the unit as a whole are listed first, followed by the performance criteria and range statements for each element.

Unit 1: Recording Income and Receipts

What is the unit about?

This unit relates to the role of invoicing and receiving payments. The first element involves individuals in preparing and checking invoices and credit notes for goods and services supplied, coding them and entering the details in the appropriate primary records and ledger accounts. The element also requires the individual to prepare statements of account. It is expected that individuals will communicate with customers, either in response to their queries or when chasing payments, and these should be handled both politely and effectively.

The second element is concerned with checking and recording receipts. The element requires the individual to deal with receipts in a variety of different forms and, therefore, to complete paying-in documents where necessary. The individual is required to deal with unusual features relating to wrongly completed cheques, out-of-date cheque, debit or credit cards, exceeded credit limits and disagreement with supporting documentation. Where these features are outside of the individual's own area of responsibility the element expects the individual to refer them to their manager or the accountant.

Knowledge and understanding

The business environment

- Types of business transactions and documents involved (Element 1.1)

- Basic law relating to contract law, sales of goods act and document retention policies (Element 1.1 & 1.2)

- General principles of VAT (Element 1.1)

- Types of discounts (Element 1.1)

- Cheques, including crossings and endorsements (Element 1.2)

- The use of banking documentation (Element 1.2)

- Automated payments: CHAPS, BACS, Direct Debits, Standing Orders (Element 1.2)

- Credit and debit cards (Element 1.2)

Accounting methods

- Double entry bookkeeping (Elements 1.1 & 1.2)

- Methods of coding data (Element 1.1)

- Operation of manual and computerised accounting systems (Elements 1.1 & 1.2)

- Batch control (Element 1.1)

- Relationship between accounting system and the ledger (Elements 1.1 & 1.2)

- Credit card procedures (Element 1.2)

- Methods of handling and storing money, including the security aspects (Element 1.2)

- Petty cash procedures: imprest and non imprest methods; analysis of receipts (Element 1.2)

The organisation

- Relevant understanding of the organisation's accounting systems and administrative systems and procedures (Elements 1.1 & 1.2)

- The nature of the organisation's business transactions (Elements 1.1 & 1.2)

- Organisational procedures for authorisation and coding of sales invoices (Element 1.1)

- Organisational procedures for filing source information (Elements 1.1 & 1.2)

- House style for correspondence (Element 1.1)

- Banking and personal security procedures (Element 1.2)

Element 1.1 Process Documents Relating to Goods and Services Supplied

Performance criteria

1 Invoices and credit notes are prepared in accordance with organisational requirements and checked against source documents

2 Calculations on invoices and credit notes are checked for accuracy

3 Invoices and credit notes are correctly authorised and coded before being sent to customers

4 Invoices and credit notes are entered into primary records according to organisational procedures

5 Entries are coded and recorded in the appropriate ledger

6 Statements of account are prepared and sent to debtors

7 Communications with customers regarding accounts are handled politely and effectively using the relevant source documents

Range statement

1 Source documents: quotations; purchase orders; delivery notes; sales orders

2 Calculations: pricing; price extensions; discounts; VAT

3 Primary records: sales daybook; sales journal; returns daybook

4 Ledger: main ledger; subsidiary ledger; integrated ledger

5 Communications: in response to queries; chasing payments

6 Source documents: aged debtors analysis

Element 1.2 Receive and Record Receipts

Performance criteria

1 Receipts are checked against relevant supporting information

2 Receipts are entered in appropriate accounting records

3 Paying-in documents are correctly prepared and reconciled to relevant records

4 Unusual features are identified and either resolved or referred to the appropriate person

Range statement

1 Receipts: cash; cheques; automated payments

2 Accounting records: cash book

3 Unusual features: wrongly completed cheques; out-of-date cheque, credit and debit cards; limits exceeded; disagreement with supporting documentation; under payments; over payments; cheques returned to sender

ASSESSMENT STRATEGY

This unit is assessed by **devolved assessment.**

Devolved assessment

Devolved assessment is a means of collecting evidence of your ability to **carry out practical activities** and to **operate effectively in the conditions of the workplace** to the standards required. Evidence may be collected at your place of work, or at an Approved Assessment Centre by means of simulations of workplace activity, or by a combination of these methods.

If the Approved Assessment Centre is a **workplace**, you may be observed carrying out accounting activities as part of your normal work routine. You should collect documentary evidence of the work you have done, or contributed to, in an **accounting portfolio**. Evidence collected in a portfolio can be assessed in addition to observed performance or where it is not possible to assess by observation.

Where the Approved Assessment Centre is a **college or training organisation**, devolved assessment will be by means of a combination of the following.

- Documentary evidence of activities carried out at the workplace, collected by you in an **accounting portfolio.**

- Realistic **simulations** of workplace activities. These simulations may take the form of case studies and in-tray exercises and involve the use of primary documents and reference sources.

- **Projects and assignments** designed to assess the Standards of Competence.

If you are unable to provide workplace evidence you will be able to complete the assessment requirements by the alternative methods listed above.

Possible assessment methods

Where possible, evidence should be collected in the workplace, but this may not be a practical prospect for you. Equally, where workplace evidence can be gathered it may not cover all elements. The AAT regards performance evidence from simulations, case studies, projects and assignments as an acceptable substitute for performance at work, provided that they are based on the Standards and, as far as possible, on workplace practice.

There are a number of methods of assessing accounting competence. The list below is not exhaustive, nor is it prescriptive. Some methods have limited applicability, but others are capable of being expanded to provide challenging tests of competence.

Assessment method	Suitable for assessing
Performance of an accounting task either in the workplace or by simulation: eg preparing and processing documents, posting entries, making adjustments, balancing, calculating, analysing information etc by manual or computerised processes	**Basic task competence.** Adding supplementary oral questioning may help to draw out underpinning knowledge and understanding and highlight your ability to deal with contingencies and unexpected occurrences
General case studies. These are broader than simulations. They include more background information about the system and business environment	Ability to **analyse a system** and suggest ways of modifying it. It could take the form of a written report, with or without the addition of oral or written questions
Accounting problems/cases: eg a list of balances that require adjustments and the preparation of final accounts	Understanding of the **general principles of accounting** as applied to a particular case or topic
Preparation of flowcharts/diagrams. To illustrate an actual (or simulated) accounting procedure	**Understanding of the logic** behind a procedure, of controls, and of relationships between departments and procedures. Questions on the flow chart or diagram can provide evidence of underpinning knowledge and understanding
Interpretation of accounting information from an actual or simulated situation. The assessment could include non-financial information and written or oral questioning	**Interpretative competence**
Preparation of written reports on an actual or simulated situation	**Written communication skills**
Analysis of critical incidents, problems encountered, achievements	Your ability to handle **contingencies**
Listing of likely errors eg preparing a list of the main types of errors likely to occur in an actual or simulated procedure	Appreciation of the range of **contingencies** likely to be encountered. Oral or written questioning would be a useful supplement to the list
Outlining the organisation's policies, guidelines and regulations	Performance criteria relating to these aspects of competence. It also provides evidence of competence in **researching information**
Objective tests and short-answer questions	**Specific knowledge**
In-tray exercises	Your **task-management ability** as well as technical competence
Supervisors' reports	**General job competence,** personal effectiveness, reliability, accuracy, and time management. Reports need to be related specifically to the Standards of Competence

Assessment method	Suitable for assessing
Analysis of work logbooks/diaries	**Personal effectiveness**, time management etc. It may usefully be supplemented with oral questioning
Oral questioning	**Knowledge and understanding** across the range of competence including organisational procedures, methods of dealing with unusual cases, contingencies and so on. It is often used in conjunction with other methods

BPP PUBLISHING

Practice devolved assessments

Practice devolved assessment
1   *Conway*

Performance criteria

The following performance criteria are covered in this Devolved Assessment.

Element 1.1 Process documents relating to goods and services supplied

4   Invoices and credit notes are entered into primary records according to organisational procedures

5   Entries are coded and recorded in the appropriate ledger

Element 1.2 Receive and record receipts

1   Receipts are entered in appropriate accounting records

Notes on completing the Assessment

This Assessment involves carrying out a bank reconciliation after posting the entries to a cash book. The cash book is run both manually and on computer. Students with access to a computer can perform the Assessment using a computerised accounting package, although some modification of the question may be necessary. Students without access to a computer should post the cash book manually and carry on with the bank reconciliation. The solution is given in both computerised and manual format.

You are allowed 2 hours to complete your work

A high level of accuracy is required. Check your work carefully.

Correcting fluid may be used but should be used in moderation. Errors should be crossed out neatly and clearly. You should write in black ink and not in pencil.

A full answer to this Assessment is provided on page 113 of this Kit.

Do not turn to the answer until you have completed all parts of the Assessment.

PRACTICE DEVOLVED ASSESSMENT 1: CONWAY

Data

Conway Ltd was incorporated five years ago. The company specialises in designing, stocking and developing gardens, usually those associated with large estates and houses. The company employs 30 people and the number of clients at any one time never exceeds six. The company uses only a dozen suppliers for garden materials, plants, trees and so on.

The company has expanded quite rapidly over the last few years and it has been decided that a computer would help to deal with stock control, salaries, the cash book and sundry other matters. The computer will be run in parallel with the manual system for three months as a check on the effectiveness and accuracy of the computer.

The low numbers of suppliers and customers mean that a complex accounting package is not considered necessary, particularly as customers change completely from year to year. The suppliers and customers have been assigned individual codes in the nominal ledger, rather than in separate sales and purchase ledgers. Invoices and credit notes are posted directly into these accounts and payments and receipts are recorded through the cash book. VAT is accounted for in the cash book for all receipts and payments *except for* the transactions with *suppliers* and *customers* (who have individual accounts in the nominal ledger).

Banking takes place at the end of each day, so all receipts for one day are banked together. All receipts and most payments are by cheque unless otherwise stated.

Tasks

Using the information and documents on the following pages, complete the tasks outlined below for July 20X5.

(a)   Using the computerised cash book, post all receipts shown for July, using the correct nominal codes and extracting the VAT where necessary.

(b)   Using the manual analysed cash book page, post the receipts shown for July excluding the VAT where necessary.

(c)   Perform a bank reconciliation for the account as at 31 July 20X5, showing all reconciling items, using the bank statements available.

(d)   In light of the results of the bank reconciliation, note:

(i)   Any corrections which must be made to the cash book
(ii)   Any matters which should be raised with the bank

Note: VAT should be rounded up or down to the nearest penny.

Documents for use in the solution

Documents which are required in the solution are:

(a)   Examples of computer screens for cash receipts
(b)   Blank manual cash book pages (receipts)

Computer screens

The following screen is an example of the type of information required in a computerised cash book.

(1)

System XX4 BANK RECEIPTS 31 July 20X5

N/C Name: BANK CURRENT ACCOUNT   Tax rate:
Batch Total:

N/C DEP	DATE	CHEQUE DETAILS	Net amount	Tax amount	Gross amount

BPP
PUBLISHING

Manual cash book: receipts

JULY - RECEIPTS

Date		Total	VAT	Sales Credit	Sales Sundry	Rent	Sundry	Fixed Assets
1 July	Brought forward	28,742 45						
2								
3								
4								
5								
6								
7								
8								
9								
10								
11								
12								
13								
14								
15								
16								
17								
18								
19								
20								
21								
22								

Cash transactions in July 20X5

The cash transactions in July 20X5 and other relevant information are listed under the following headings.

(a) Balance brought forward, and outstanding items
(b) Receipts
(c) Nominal ledger codes
(d) Bank statements for July 20X5

Balance brought forward

The balance in the cash book at the end of 30 June 20X5 (and after any corrections) was £28,742.45 DR.

The following items were listed as reconciling items in the bank reconciliations carried out as at 30 June 20X5.

Cheques outstanding (all 20X5)

		£
January 4	110204	29.42
June 8	113643	59.75
June 16	113710	158.05
June 29	113721	456.25
June 29	113722	507.30
June 30	113723	88.41

Outstanding lodgements (receipts)

		£
June 29	Cheques banked	3,271.87
		4,115.60
		2,007.31

Receipts: July 20X5

Date	Payee and details	Amount received £	VAT rate %
1.7.X5	Fernlea Manor: payment 7	2,960.88	17.5
1.7.X5	M Parr: sale of car	5,000.00	-
3.7.X5	Levison House: payment 3	1,284.74	17.5
4.7.X5	Blackwood Park Estates: payment 10	8,619.03	17.5
9.7.X5	Elliott Grange: payment 1	8,585.52	17.5
9.7.X5	Portmans: payment 6	6,986.82	17.5
12.7.X5	Inland Revenue: tax rebate	579.26	-
12.7.X5	Sale of excess small plants to public	1,427.82	17.5
16.7.X5	Electricity Board: rebate	72.50	17.5
19.7.X5	Brokers Inc: sale of shares	3,247.92	-
19.7.X5	Rent: Hunt Lodge	7,500.00	-
24.7.X5	Elliot Grange: payment 2	2,712.53	17.5
25.7.X5	Banner-Crittel: payment 4	8,229.09	17.5
29.7.X5	Portmans: payment 7	9,201.67	17.5
29.7.X5	Blackwood Park Estate: final payment 11	31,572.84	17.5
29.7.X5	Fernlea Manor: payment 8	8,485.08	17.5
30.7.X5	Levison House: payment 5	6,898.69	17.5
30.7.X5	Blackwood Park Estate: excess charge	2,471.20	17.5

Nominal ledger codes

1000	Bank
1100	VAT
3410	Blackwood Park Estates
3420	Fernlea Manor
3430	Portmans
3440	Banner-Crittel
3450	Levison House
3460	Elliot Grange
5670	General/sundry
5780	Rent (income)
5800	Sales
7230	Freehold property
7240	Sundry debtors

Summary

3400 - 3799	Customer codes (debtors)
4100 - 4499	Supplier codes (creditors)
5500 - 5999	Expense/revenue codes
7200 - 7299	Asset codes
7400 - 7599	Liability codes

Bank statements

Studio Bank
CONFIDENTIAL

5 High Street
Guildford
Surrey

Account   Conway Ltd
Hilltop Farm
Godalming
Surrey

SHEET NO	66

Telephone 01244 472318

1995   Statement date   7 July 20X5   Account no   1443277

Date	Details		Withdrawals	Deposits	Balance (£)
1 July	Balance from sheet no.	65			20,646.85
2 July	Charges		448.21		
		113643	59.75		
		113710	158.05		
	CC			9,394.78	29,375.62
3 July	CC			7,960.88	37,336.50
5 July	CC			1,284.74	
		113721	456.25		
		113722	507.30		37,657.69
7 July	CC			8,619.03	
		113723	88.41		
		113726	12,840.33		33,347.98
7 July	Balance to Sheet no.	67			33,347.98

Key	**SO** Standing Order	**DV** Dividend	**CC** Cash &/or Cheques	**AW** Auto withdrawals	**PY** Payroll	**Interest** -see over
	EC Eurocheque	**TR** Transfer	**CP** Card Purchases	**DD** Direct Debit	**OD** Overdrawn	

Studio Bank

CONFIDENTIAL

5 High Street
Guildford
Surrey

Account   Conway Ltd
Hilltop Farm
Godalming
Surrey

SHEET NO	67

Telephone   01244 472318

1995   Statement date   15 July 20X5   Account no   1443277

Date	Details	Withdrawals	Deposits	Balance (£)
7 July	Balance from sheet no. 66			33,347.98
8 July	113724	335.71		
	113725	4,425.78		
	113728	650.00		27,936.49
9 July	113727	3,056.36		24,880.13
13 July	CC		15,572.34	40,452.47
14 July	113729	95.82		
	113730	95.82		
	113729	95.82		40,165.01
15 July	113733	21,567.45		
	113735	8,974.16		9,623.40
15 July	Balance to Sheet no. 68			9,623.40

Key	**SO** Standing Order	**DV** Dividend	**CC** Cash &/or Cheques	**AW** Auto withdrawals	**PY** Payroll	**Interest** -see over
	EC Eurocheque	**TR** Transfer	**CP** Card Purchases	**DD** Direct Debit	**OD** Overdrawn	

Studio Bank

CONFIDENTIAL

5 High Street
Guildford
Surrey

Account   Conway Ltd
Hilltop Farm
Godalming
Surrey

SHEET NO	68

Telephone   01244 472318

1995   Statement date   23 July 20X5   Account no   1443277

Date	Details	Withdrawals	Deposits	Balance (£)
15 July	Balance from sheet no. 67			9,623.40
16 July	CC		2,007.08	
	113731	3,492.01		
	113732	839.29		
	113734	87.13		7,212.05
17 July	SO	185.20		7,026.85
20 July	SO Rebate		72.50	
	113738	5,697.05		
	113739	220.06		1,182.24
21 July	DD Water	332.29		849.95
22 July	113737	1,248.59		398.64 **OD**
23 July	CC		10,747.92	10,349.28
23 July	Balance to Sheet no. 69			10,349.28

Key	**SO** Standing Order	**DV** Dividend	**CC** Cash &/or Cheques	**AW** Auto withdrawals	**PY** Payroll	**Interest** -see over
	EC Eurocheque	**TR** Transfer	**CP** Card Purchases	**DD** Direct Debit	**OD** Overdrawn	

Studio Bank

CONFIDENTIAL

5 High Street
Guildford
Surrey

Account Conway Ltd
Hilltop Farm
Godalming
Surrey

SHEET NO   69

Telephone 01244 472318

1995   Statement date   31 July 20X5   Account no   1443277

Date	Details	Withdrawals	Deposits	Balance (£)
23 July	Balance from sheet no. 68			10,349.28
24 July	113742	120.47		10,228.81
27 July	Unauthorised OD Fee	150.00		
	CC		2,712.53	12,791.34
28 July	113742	120.47		
	CC		8,229.09	20,899.96
29 July	113744	258.94		20,641.02
30 July	BACS Salaries	31,721.82		
	DD Rates	417.60		11,498.40 **OD**
31 July	Balance to Sheet no. 70			11,498.40 **OD**

Key	**SO** Standing Order	**DV** Dividend	**CC** Cash &/or Cheques	**AW** Auto withdrawals	**PY** Payroll	**Interest** -see over
	EC Eurocheque	**TR** Transfer	**CP** Card Purchases	**DD** Direct Debit	**OD** Overdrawn	

Practice devolved assessment
2 *Apparat*

Performance criteria

The following performance criteria are covered in this Devolved Assessment.

Element 1.1 Process documents relating to goods and services supplied

1   Invoices and credit notes are prepared in accordance with organisational requirements and checked against source documents

2   Calculations on invoices and credit notes are checked for accuracy

3   Invoices and credit notes are correctly authorised and coded before being sent to customers

4   Invoices and credit notes are entered into primary records according to organisational procedures

5   Entries are coded and recorded in the appropriate ledger

6   Statements of account are prepared and sent to debtors

7   Communications with customers regarding accounts are handled politely and effectively using the relevant source documents

Element 1.2 Receive and record receipts

1   Receipts are checked against relevant supporting information

2   Receipts are entered in appropriate accounting records

3   Paying-in documents are correctly prepared and reconciled to relevant records

4   Unusual features are identified and either resolved or referred to the appropriate person

Notes on completing the Assessment

This Assessment is designed to test your ability to post transactions correctly to the sales accounts, prepare customer sales statements and an aged debtors analysis and communicate with debtors.

You are allowed 2 hours to complete your work.

A high level of accuracy is required. Check your work carefully.

Correcting fluid may be used but should be used in moderation. Errors should be crossed out neatly and clearly. You should write in black ink and not in pencil.

A full answer to this Assessment is provided on page 117 of this Kit.

Do not turn to the answer until you have completed all parts of the Assessment.

This Assessment can be performed either manually or using a PC equipped with a sales ledger program and printer

PRACTICE DEVOLVED ASSESSMENT 2: APPARAT

Data

Jill Regan has set up a business, Apparat Ltd, which sells office and classroom equipment to other businesses, and to the general public. The company does not itself carry out installation work for the equipment it sells. Some of its sales are made for cash, particularly those to the general public. However, Jill also offers 30-day credit terms. The company first traded on 4 June 20X5 and is registered for value added tax. Sales of all of the company's products are treated as taxable supplies at the standard VAT rate of 17½%.

It is now 3 September 20X5 and you have started work as an assistant to Jill. Apparat Ltd has traded on credit terms with six customers since trading began. Jill now wants to process the transactions on the sales ledger. When you ask what credit limit each customer is allocated, Jill tells you that the limit is £1,000 for each customer except for Sedgedown Borough Council, which has a credit limit of £3,000, Sada Ltd, which has a credit limit of £2,500, and Babbage & Lovelace, who have a credit limit of £500.

Customer details are as follows.

St James Comprehensive School, Kirk Avenue, Sedgedown SD1 7PP
Siward Ltd, 39 Telford Way, Ocset SD3 9DA
Education Department, Sedgedown Borough Council, 24 Meadsway, Sedgedown SD1 2NE
Sada Ltd, Unit 33, Sedgedown Business Park, Trowse Way, Sedgedown SD2 1PA
Graham Light (Projects) Ltd, 24A High Street, Ribben Village, Sedgedown SD7 4NO
Babbage & Lovelace, 2 Telford Way, Ocset, SD3 9DA

The following customer transactions have occurred. The amounts shown for sales *exclude* value added tax.

June
6	Goods £670.00 sold to St James Comprehensive School, invoice 1001.
8	Goods £420.00 sold to Siward Ltd, invoice 1002.
14	Goods £700.00 sold to Sada Ltd, invoice 1003.
18	Goods £700.00 sold to Graham Light (Projects) Ltd, invoice 1004.
19	Credit note 9001 for £350.00 plus VAT issued to Sada Ltd, as some of goods sold on 14 June were faulty.
25	Goods £44.00 sold to St James Comprehensive School, invoice 1005.
28	Goods £88.00 sold to Sedgedown Borough Council, invoice 1006.

July
2	Goods £210.00 sold to Siward Ltd, invoice 1007.
3	Cheque for £838.95 received from St James Comprehensive School.
11	Goods £350.00 sold to Sada Ltd, invoice 1008.
18	Goods £540.00 sold to Babbage & Lovelace, invoice 1009.
23	Credit note 9002 for £540.00 plus VAT issued to Babbage & Lovelace, as goods supplied on 18 July were faulty.
24	Goods £790 sold to Siward Ltd, invoice 1010.
27	Goods £540.00 sold to Babbage & Lovelace, invoice 1011.
25	Cheque for £103.40 received from Sedgedown Borough Council.
26	Cheque for £411.25 received from Sada Ltd.
30	Goods £2,500.00 sold to Sedgedown Borough council, invoice 1012.
30	Goods £90.00 sold to St James Comprehensive School, invoice 1013.
30	Goods £90.00 sold to Babbage & Lovelace, invoice 1014.

August
2	Cheque for £300.00 received from Babbage & Lovelace.
8	Goods £180.00 sold to St James Comprehensive School, invoice 1015.
9	Goods £50.00 sold to Babbage & Lovelace, invoice 1016.
15	Goods £150.00 sold to Sada Ltd, invoice 1017.
17	Credit note 9003 for £500.00 plus VAT issued to Sedgedown Borough Council.
20	Goods £100.00 sold to Sada Ltd, invoice 1018.
22	Goods £90.00 sold to St James Comprehensive School, invoice 1019.
24	Cheque for £105.75 received from St James Comprehensive School.
24	Cheque for £2,350.00 received from Sedgedown Borough Council.
27	Cheque for £668.50 received from Siward Ltd.
27	Goods £1,250.00 sold to Sedgedown Borough Council, invoice 1020.
29	Goods £240 sold to Sedgedown Borough Council, invoice 1021.
29	Goods £26.00 sold to Graham Light (Projects) Ltd, invoice 1022.

Tasks

If you are using a microcomputer equipment with a sales ledger program and a printer, follow the instructions below for parts (a) to (e) of the Assessment. If you are carrying out the Assessment without a microcomputer, follow the alternative instructions given.

(a) Open accounts for each of Apparat Ltd's customers, using the microcomputer sales ledger program.

(b) Enter the transactions for June 20X5 and July 20X5. Provided that you input the correct VAT rate, the computer program will calculate the VAT for you.

(c) Print out customer statements and an aged debtors' listing as at the end of July 20X5.

(d) Enter the transactions for August 20X5.

(e) Print out customer statements and an aged debtors listing as at the end of August 20X5.

Alternative instructions for parts (a) to (e) using manual processing are as follows.

(a) Rule up columns for the accounts of Apparat Ltd's customers.

(b) Open each account with a nil balance as at 4 June 20X5.

(c) Enter the transactions in the sales ledger accounts opened in (a) for each of the months June 20X5, July 20X5 and August 20X5, balancing each active account at each month end.

(d) Complete statements of account as at 31 August 20X5 for each of the customers. Proformas are given below. Payments are to be matched with the oldest items on the account. Statements of account are to itemise all outstanding items, and all transactions in the month of the statement.

(e) Prepare an aged debtors' listing as at the end of August 20X5.

Parts (f) and (g) of the Assessment are common to both approaches.

(f) Jill tells you that she is concerned that action should be taken to make sure that customers pay on time. She is also concerned that you check on the August age analysis that all credit limits are being adhered to. Prepare a memorandum addressed to Jill explaining what action should be taken in respect of slow payers and commenting on the payment performance of debtors and credit limits during the first three months of trading.

(g)   Draft any letters to send to debtors which are necessary in order to implement the actions which you propose in (f). Letters should be addressed to the Finance Director of debtor companies, or other appropriate officials, and are to be signed by Jill Regan as Managing Director.

Documents for use in the solution

The documents you will need to prepare a solution are given on the following pages and consist of customer statements of account.

STATEMENT OF ACCOUNT

Apparat Ltd, 7A Meadsway, Sedgedown SD1 2ND. Tel/Fax: 01664-24274
VAT Reg No: 01 424 4288
Customer name:
Address:

Date	Description/reference	Debit £ p	Credit £ p	Balance £ p
AMOUNT NOW DUE				

Registered Office: 7A Meadsway, Sedgedown, SD1 2ND. Reg No. 18018047

STATEMENT OF ACCOUNT

Apparat Ltd, 7A Meadsway, Sedgedown SD1 2ND. Tel/Fax: 01664-24274
VAT Reg No: 01 424 4288
Customer name:
Address:

Date	Description/reference	Debit £ p	Credit £ p	Balance £ p
AMOUNT NOW DUE				

Registered Office: 7A Meadsway, Sedgedown, SD1 2ND. Reg No. 18018047

BPP
PUBLISHING

STATEMENT OF ACCOUNT

Apparat Ltd, 7A Meadsway, Sedgedown SD1 2ND. Tel/Fax: 01664-24274
VAT Reg No: 01 424 4288
Customer name:
Address:

Date	Description/reference	Debit £ p	Credit £ p	Balance £ p
AMOUNT NOW DUE				

Registered Office: 7A Meadsway, Sedgedown, SD1 2ND. Reg No. 18018047

STATEMENT OF ACCOUNT

Apparat Ltd, 7A Meadsway, Sedgedown SD1 2ND. Tel/Fax: 01664-24274
VAT Reg No: 01 424 4288
Customer name:
Address:

Date	Description/reference	Debit £ p	Credit £ p	Balance £ p
AMOUNT NOW DUE				

Registered Office: 7A Meadsway, Sedgedown, SD1 2ND. Reg No. 18018047

STATEMENT OF ACCOUNT

Apparat Ltd, 7A Meadsway, Sedgedown SD1 2ND. Tel/Fax: 01664-24274
VAT Reg No: 01 424 4288
Customer name:
Address:

Date	Description/reference	Debit £ p	Credit £ p	Balance £ p
AMOUNT NOW DUE				

Registered Office: 7A Meadsway, Sedgedown, SD1 2ND. Reg No. 18018047

STATEMENT OF ACCOUNT

Apparat Ltd, 7A Meadsway, Sedgedown SD1 2ND. Tel/Fax: 01664-24274
VAT Reg No: 01 424 4288
Customer name:
Address:

Date	Description/reference	Debit £ p	Credit £ p	Balance £ p
AMOUNT NOW DUE				

Registered Office: 7A Meadsway, Sedgedown, SD1 2ND. Reg No. 18018047

Trial run devolved assessments

TRIAL RUN DEVOLVED ASSESSMENT 1

FOUNDATION STAGE - NVQ/SVQ2

Unit 1

Recording Income and Receipts

The purpose of this Trial Run Devolved Assessment is to give you an idea of what an AAT simulation looks like. It is not intended as a definitive guide to the tasks you may be required to perform.

The suggested time allowance for this Assessment is **four hours,** two hours for Part 1 and two hours for Part 2. Up to 30 minutes extra time may be permitted in an AAT simulation. Breaks in assessment will be allowed in the AAT simulation, but it must normally be completed in one day.

Calculators may be used but no reference material is permitted.

**DO NOT OPEN THIS PAPER UNTIL YOU ARE READY TO START
UNDER TIMED CONDITIONS**

PART 1 - BARKERS

INSTRUCTIONS

This Assessment is designed to test your ability to record and account for income and receipts.

The situation is provided on Page 23.

The tasks you are to perform are set out on Page 24.

You are provided with data on Pages 25 to 28 which you must use to complete the tasks.

Your answers should be set out in the answer booklet on Pages 29 to 38 using the documents provided. You may require additional answer pages.

You are allowed two hours to complete your work.

A high level of accuracy is required. Check your work carefully.

Correcting fluid may be used but should be used in mdoeration. Errors should be crossed out neatly and clearly. You should write in black ink, not pencil.

You are advised to read the whole of the Assessment before commencing as all of the information may be of value and is not necessarily supplied in the sequence in which you might wish to deal with it.

A full answer to this Assessment is provided on Page 128 of this Kit.

SITUATION

Barkers Ltd was set up about ten years ago by George 'Bulldog' Barker to manufacture and sell dog kennels to both trade and retail customers.

There is a small shop/office attached to the company's factory in Dalmatian Road, Wagford. Barker's extensive range of kennels is on display in the shop and retail customers are welcome to browse and buy.

'Bulldog' Barker still owns and manages the company. As well as the four men who work in the factory, there are seven other members of staff. The finance director, Mr Bone, oversees the work of the bookkeeper/shop assistant, Lassie McDonald and you, Rex Cash, the accounts clerk. Mr Marrow, the sales director, has one sales person, Winifred Anne Lot, working for her. (Winifred prefers to be called Win.) Pat Pant, the purchasing clerk, reports to Mrs Growler, the purchases director.

Receipts in any day consist of cash, cheques and credit cards from retail sales, which are put through an electronic cash register and placed for safe keeping in a safe on the premises at night. Statements to trade customers are sent out towards the end of each month and trade customers usually send cheque payments a couple of days later. Credit customers may take advantage of a 5% discount if they pay within seven days of the invoice date. Any cheques received from trade customers are entered on a cheque listing by Lassie.

Lassie runs a manual cash book to which she posts payments and receipts at the end of each month. After balancing off the cash book, she prepares a reconciliation statement between the cash book and the bank statement. She is also responsible for petty cash.

The company is registered for VAT. All sales are standard rated unless stated otherwise.

Lassie has taken a holiday to the Isle of Skye and so you have been asked to carry out the month-end procedures. She has delegated to you her responsibilities and powers, for example, authorisation.

BPP PUBLISHING

THE TASKS TO BE PERFORMED

In the answer booklet on Pages 29 to 38 complete the tasks outlined below for April 1995 month-end procedures. Data for this assessment is provided on Pages 25 to 28.

1 Assume that the cheques received from credit customers agree to the remittance advices. Prepare a cheque listing for the cheques received from credit customers.

2 Record the credit card sales on the credit card summary voucher.

3 Prepare a paying-in slip to bank the cheques received from trade customers and the credit card vouchers, cheques and cash receipts from retail sales (ignore the breakdown of cash).

4 Prepare the receipts side of the cash book for April on a weekly summary basis, analysing receipts from cheque, cash and credit card retail sales receipts, and receipts from trade sales. (You can find the balance brought forward at 1 April elsewhere in this assessment.)

5 Post the totals to the nominal ledger accounts on Pages 35 to 37. Balance off the ledger accounts and carry forward balances.

6 Using the information in the reconciliation prepared by Lassie at the end of March 20X5, prepare a reconciliation between the cash book and bank statement at 30 April 20X5.

Note: VAT should be rounded up or down to the nearest penny.

DATA

(a) The following remittance advices (with cheques) were received from credit customers on 1 May 20X5.

S8773

REMITTANCE ADVICE

POOCHY   PET   SHOP
POODLE   LANE
YAPPINGTON

TO: BARKERS   LIMITED
DALMATION   ROAD
WAGFORD

| Account Ref | P009 | Date | 28/4/X5 | Page | 1 |

DATE	DETAILS		INVOICES	CREDIT NOTES	PAYMENT AMOUNT
5.4.X5	Invoice	1139	199.50		199.50
15.4.X5	Invoice	1145	376.42		376.42
16.4.X5	Invoice	1146	500.00		500.00
19.4.X5	Credit note (inv 1127) 73			112.15	-112.15
29.4.X5	Invoice	1156	307.06		307.06
	Discount at 5%			15.35	-15.35
			1,382.98	127.50	1,255.48

S8774

REMITTANCE ADVICE

IT'S A DOG'S LIFE
ROVER ROAD
COLLYFORD

TO: BARKERS   LIMITED
DALMATION   ROAD
WAGFORD

| Account Ref | I008 | Date | 28/4/X5 | Page | 1 |

DATE	DETAILS		INVOICES	CREDIT NOTES	PAYMENT AMOUNT
5.4.X5	Invoice	1140	17.50		17.50
22.4.X5	Invoice	1151	42.99		42.99
24.4.X5	Invoice	1152	53.30		53.30
25.4.X5	Credit note (inv 1139) 75			40.21	-40.21
27.4.X5	Invoice	1155	17.50		17.50
28.4.X5	Credit note (Inv 1133) 76			7.60	-7.60
	Discount at 5%			3.54	-3.54
			131.29	51.35	79.94

BPP PUBLISHING

S8775

REMITTANCE ADVICE

PET SUPERSTORE
TERRIER STREET
YORK

TO: BARKERS LIMITED
DALMATION ROAD
WAGFORD

| Account Ref | P013 | Date | 29/4/X5 | Page | 1 |

DATE	DETAILS		INVOICES	CREDIT NOTES	PAYMENT AMOUNT
6.4.X5	Invoice	1141	37.50		37.50
9.4.X5	Invoice	1142	119.21		119.21
10.4.X5	Invoice	1143	42.99		42.99
17.4.X5	Invoice	1147	17.50		17.50
20.4.X5	Invoice	1148	21.66		21.66
24.4.X5	Invoice	1153	21.66		21.66
24.4.X5	Credit note (inv 1121)	74		75.61	-75.61
27.4.X5	Invoice	1154	21.66		21.66
	Discount at 5%			2.17	-2.17
			282.18	77.78	204.40

S8776

REMITTANCE ADVICE

PET PARLOUR
DOBERMAN ROAD
WAGFORD

TO: BARKERS LIMITED
DALMATION ROAD
WAGFORD

| Account Ref | P027 | Date | 29/4/X5 | Page | 1 |

DATE	DETAILS		INVOICES	CREDIT NOTES	PAYMENT AMOUNT
11.4.X5	Invoice	1144	221.50		221.50
21.4.X5	Invoice	1149	572.60		572.60
22.4.X5	Invoice	1150	32.90		32.90
			827.00		827.00

(b) Retail sales receipts during the month are set out below.

Week	Cash £	Credit cards £		Cheques £
1	130.70	33.50	Mrs I Whippet	17.50
		170.90	Mr J Corgi	22.99
		12.99	Miss L Scott	13.99
		21.50		
2	98.50	42.50	Mr and Mrs N Hound	13.50
		17.99	Miss A Mutt	17.68
		10.99		
3	572.60	22.99	Mr B Pup	50.00
4	13.99	11.50		
		49.99		

(c) This bank statement covers April 20X5.

Crufts Bank

CONFIDENTIAL

20 Spillers Lane
Wagford

Account Barkers Ltd
Dalmation Road
Wagford

SHEET NO   79

Telephone   01729 35272

20X5

Statement date   1 May 20X5

Account no   30595713

Date	Details		Withdrawals	Deposits	Balance (£)
1 April	Balance from Sheet no.	78			5140.77
3 April		101095	13.99		
		101097	72.50		5054.28
4 April	CC			1351.21	6405.49
5 April		101093	45.21		6360.28
10 April		101099	179.60		
		101094	352.17		
		101098	55.00		5773.51
18 April	DD British Telecom		120.00		5653.51
21 April	Interest - Deposit account			79.87	5733.38
30 April	SO Doberman Mgt Co (rent)		100.00		
	DD Rates		50.00		
	BACS Salaries		1251.00		
30 April		101100	84.23		4248.15
	Balance to Sheet no.	80			4248.15

Key	**SO** Standing Order	**DV** Dividend	**CC** Cash &/or Cheques	**CGS** Charges	**PY** Payroll	**INT** Interest
	EC Eurocheque	**TR** Transfer	**CP** Card Purchases	**DD** Direct Debit	**OD** Overdrawn	**ADJ** Adjustment

(d) *Bank reconciliation at 31 March 20X5*

	£	£
Balance per bank statement		5,140.77
Add outstanding lodgements		1,351.21
Less cheques not yet presented		
101093	45.21	
101094	352.17	
101095	13.99	
101096	101.01	
101097	72.50	
101098	55.00	
101099	179.60	
		(819.48)
Balance per cash book		5,672.50

TRIAL RUN DEVOLVED ASSESSMENT 1
PART 1 - BARKERS

Recording Income and Receipts

ANSWER BOOKLET

Documents for use in this Assessment

The documents you will need to prepare the solution are given on the following pages and consist of:

(a)   A blank cheque listing

(b)   A blank credit card summary voucher

(c)   A blank paying-in slip

(d)   A blank receipts page from the cash book

(e)   Selected nominal ledger accounts

BPP
PUBLISHING

(a) Cheques received listing

CHEQUE LISTING		BARKERS LIMITED	
	DATE		20
NAME		ACCOUNT	AMOUNT
TOTAL			

(b) Credit card summary voucher

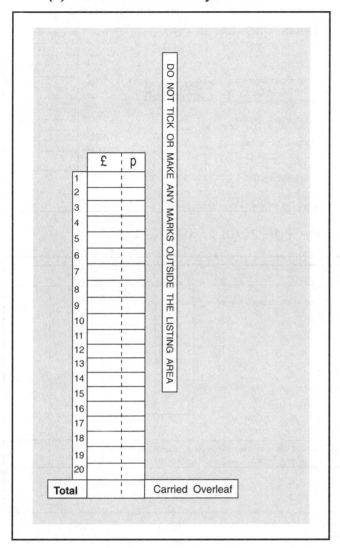

	£	p
1		
2		
3		
4		
5		
6		
7		
8		
9		
10		
11		
12		
13		
14		
15		
16		
17		
18		
19		
20		
Total		Carried Overleaf

DO NOT TICK OR MAKE ANY MARKS OUTSIDE THE LISTING AREA

HAVE YOU IMPRINTED THE SUMMARY WITH YOUR RETAILER'S CARD?

BANK Processing (White) copy of
Summary with your Vouchers in
correct order:
1. SUMMARY
2. SALES VOUCHERS
3. REFUND VOUCHERS
KEEP Retailer's copies (Blue & Yellow)
NO MORE THAN 200 Vouchers to each
Summary
DO NOT USE Staples, Pins, Paper Clips

	ITEMS	AMOUNT	
SALES VOUCHERS (LISTED OVERLEAF)			
LESS REFUND VOUCHERS			
DATE	TOTAL		:

SUMMARY - RETAILER'S COPY

Crufts Bank
FASTPASS

**BANKING
SUMMARY**

- - - - - - - - - - - - - - - -
RETAILER'S SIGNATURE

COMPLETE THIS SUMMARY FOR EVERY DEPOSIT OF SALES VOUCHERS AND ENTER THE
TOTAL ON YOUR NORMAL CURRENT ACCOUNT PAYING-IN SLIP

BPP PUBLISHING

(c) Paying-in slip

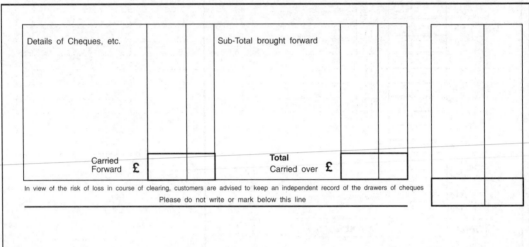

(d) Manual cash book: receipts

			Discounts given		Total		VAT		Debtors		Cash Sales		Other receipts	
APRIL - RECEIPTS														
1														
2														
3														
4														
5														
6														
7														
8														
9														
10														
11														
12														
13														
14														
15														
16														
17														
18														
19														
20														
21														
22														

(e) Nominal ledger accounts

Debtors control account

Date	Details	Amount	Date	Details	Amount
		£			£
1 April 20X5	Balance b/f	Nil	30 April 20X5	Sales returns day book	235.57
30 April 20X5	Sales day book	2,623.45			

Sales

Date	Details	Amount	Date	Details	Amount
		£			£
30 April 20X5	Sales returns day book	235.57	1 April 20X5	Balance b/f	6,826.30
			30 April 20X5	Sales day book	2,623.45

Bank interest received

Date	Details	Amount	Date	Details	Amount
		£			£
			1 April 20X5	Balance b/f	284.50

VAT

Date	Details	Amount	Date	Details	Amount
		£			£
30 April 20X5	Purchase day book	181 43	1 April 20X5	Balance b/f	586 48
			30 April 20X5	Sales day book	352 51

Discounts allowed

Date	Details	Amount	Date	Details	Amount
		£			£
1 April 20X5	Balance b/d	67 42			

Workings

PART 2 - BEST BOOKS

INSTRUCTIONS

This Assessment is designed to test your ability to record income and receipts.

The situation is provided on Page 40.

You are provided with data on Pages 42 to 51 which you must use to complete the related tasks on Page 41.

Your answers should be set out in this booklet using the documents provided. You may require additional answer pages.

You are allowed two hours to complete your work.

A high level of accuracy is required. Check your work carefully.

Correcting fluid may be used but should be used in moderation. Errors should be crossed out neatly and clearly. You should write in black ink, not pencil.

You are advised to read the whole of the Assessment before commencing as all of the information may be of value and is not necessarily supplied in the sequence in which you might wish to deal with it.

A full answer to this Assessment is provided on Page 135 of this Kit.

THE SITUATION

Your name is Alan Murray and you are employed as an accounts clerk, in a regional book shop, for a chain of book shops throughout the country. You are employed in the North West Regional office at 101, Blackburn Road, Preston PR1 2HE and today's date is Monday 12 May 20X7. The name of the organisation is Best-Books Ltd.

The business

The North West Regional Office co-ordinates the commercial activities of 10 book shops throughout the North of England involving a range of customers from academic institutions, college and university lecturers and individuals.

Books are zero-rated for VAT purposes.

Sales/income

You are based in the Regional Office for the North West and one of your duties is to complete the takings schedule and arrange completion of the bank paying-in information for the shop in which you are based. Individuals pay in the shop by cash, cheque or credit card. One of your tasks if to give a receipt to those customers who require one. Another task you have to undertake is the daily completion of the takings schedule for the Preston shop, and preparation of the bank paying-in slips.

Another of your duties involves reconciling cheques received from other branches with the relevant remittance advices.

Cash and bank

One of the tasks you undertake is to balance off the cash book for each of the shops within the region on a monthly basis.

THE TASKS TO BE PERFORMED

		Blank document on page(s)
1	Prepare receipts for those customers who require one (the next receipt number if R107).	42-44
2	Complete the takings schedule for Monday 12 May 20X7 noting that the float required is £30.	44
3	Complete the cash reconciliation sheet prior to banking.	45
4	You are required to complete the bank paying-in slip.	46
5	You are asked to check the cheques received from the Midlands area against the remittance advices and advise of any action o t which you may need take in respect of any of the payments received.	47-49
6	Balance the ledger accounts of A Tatlock plc and P Davies Ltd, as at 30/04/X7.	49
7	Prepare the two column cash book for the Blackpool shop for April 20X7, including carrying down the balances, at 30/04/X7.	51

BPP
PUBLISHING

DATA

Details of sales for Monday 12 May 20X7

Customer	Value of sale £	Cash/cheque/credit card
1	3.99	Cash
2★	14.51	Cash
3	10.50	Cheque
4	11.29	Cash
5	3.49	Cash
6	13.54	Cheque
7★	27.99	Cheque
8★	58.99	Cheque
9	1.99	Cash
10	26.99	Credit card
11★	14.40	Cash
12	21.90	Cheque
13	8.50	Cash
14	7.49	Cash
15	103.99	Credit card
16★	17.46	Cheque
17	71.49	Credit card
18★	11.46	Cash
19	1.99	Cash
20	64.45	Cheque

★ Those customers who required a receipt.

Best-Books Ltd	No _____ Best-Books Ltd _____ 20 _____
No _____	Received with thanks the sum of _____ pounds _____ pence cheque/cash
_____ 20 _____	
£ _____	£ _____ Signature _____

BPP PUBLISHING

Best-Books Ltd

No _____

_____ 20 _____

£ _____

No _____ Best-Books Ltd _____ 20 _____

Received with
thanks the   _____ pounds
sum of   _____ pence
                                              cheque/cash

£ _____ Signature _____

Best-Books Ltd

No _____

_____ 20 _____

£ _____

No _____ Best-Books Ltd _____ 20 _____

Received with
thanks the   _____ pounds
sum of   _____ pence
                                              cheque/cash

£ _____ Signature _____

Best-Books Ltd

No _____

_____ 20 _____

£ _____

No _____ Best-Books Ltd _____ 20 _____

Received with
thanks the   _____ pounds
sum of   _____ pence
                                              cheque/cash

£ _____ Signature _____

Best-Books Ltd

No _____

_____ 20 _____

£ _____

No _____ Best-Books Ltd _____ 20 _____

Received with
thanks the
sum of _____ pounds

_____ pence

cheque/cash

£ _____ Signature _____

Best-Books Ltd

No _____

_____ 20 _____

£ _____

No _____ Best-Books Ltd _____ 20 _____

Received with
thanks the
sum of _____ pounds

_____ pence

cheque/cash

£ _____ Signature _____

Takings schedule

PRESTON SHOP	DATE:	
	£	£
Float at start of day		
Receipts for day		
Cash		
Cheque		
Credit card	_____	
Total		
Less: Float required		
Credit card transactions		_____
Amount to be banked		_____

Cash details for Monday 12 May 20X7

| | Cash paid | | | | | | | | | | Change given | | | | | | | | | |
| | Notes | | | Coins | | | | | | | Notes | | | Coins | | | | | | |
Customer	£20	£10	£5	£1	50p	20p	10p	5p	2p	1p	£20	£10	£5	£1	50p	20p	10p	5p	2p	1p
Opening float		2	1	2	2	3	2	4	40	20										
1			1											1						1
2		1		5						1					1					
4	1												1	3	1	1				1
5				4												2	1			1
9				2																1
11		1	1			2								1						
13		1												1			1	4	10	
14			1	2	1															1
18		1		1	1															4
19				2																1

The closing float is required to be as follows.

	Number
£10 note	2
£5 note	1
£1 coin	4
50p	1
20p	1
10p	0
5p	0
2p	10
1p	10

Cash reconciliation sheet

| | Notes | | | Coins | | | | | | |
	£20	£10	£5	£1	50p	20p	10p	5p	2p	1p
Opening float										
+ Total received in day										
– Total paid in change										
– Float required										
Total to be banked										
Number										
Value £										

Bank paying-in slip

Date _____		

£50 notes		
£20 notes		
£10 notes		
£5 notes		
£1		
50p		
20p		
10p		
5p		
Bronze		
Total		
Cash		
Cheques		
(see over)		
£		

bank giro credit

Paid in by/Customer's Reference

Date _____

Code No: 30-60-58
Bank: Lancs Bank PLC
Branch: Preston

Credit: BEST BOOKS LTD
Account No: 60711348

Number
of
Cheques

Paid in by _____

£50 notes		
£20 notes		
£10 notes		
£5 notes		
£1		
50p		
20p		
10p		
5p		
Bronze		
Total		
Cash		
Cheques		
(see over)		
£		

Cheque analysis		Counterfoil	
Customer No	£	Customer No	£

Cheques received

Midlands Bank PLC

HIGH STREET, WOLVERHAMPTON

10 - 5 20 X7

29-30-36

Pay Best Books Ltd

Six hundred and

eighty four pounds 50p

Account Payee

£ 664.50p

P Davies

P DAVIES LTD

216091   293036   60449347

Walsall Bank PLC

HIGH STREET, WALSALL

8 - 5 20 X7

34-20-62

Pay Best Books Ltd

One hundred and

twenty pounds only

Account Payee

£ 120.00p

M Pagan

M PAGAN LTD

312048   342038   6166943

Coventry Bank PLC

HIGH STREET, COVENTRY

6 - 5 20 X7

26-41-38

Pay Best Books Ltd

One hundred and

ninety two pounds 40p

Account Payee

£ 192.40p

A Tatlock

A TATLOCK PLC

207943   264138   3060492

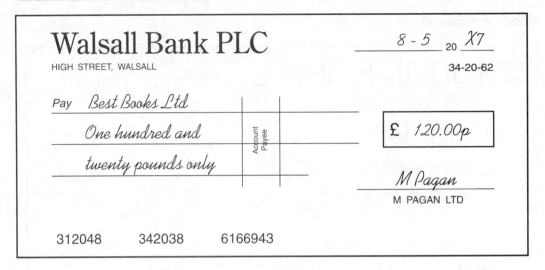

Walsall Bank PLC

HIGH STREET, WALSALL

8 - 5 20 X7

34-20-62

Pay *Best Books Ltd*

One hundred and

twenty pounds only

Account Payee

£ *120.00p*

M Pagan

M PAGAN LTD

312048   342038   6166943

Remittance advices received

Remittance Advice	
Account: P Davies Ltd	
Outstanding	*Included in cheque*
£	
153.62	✓
101.29	✓
64.08	✓
201.00	✓
84.51	✓
80.00	✓
74.30	

Remittance Advice	
Account: J Davidson Ltd	
Outstanding	*Included in cheque*
£	
63.40	✓
100.40	✓
49.30	✓
6.90	
14.25	
19.82	

Remittance Advice	
Account: A Tatlock plc	
Outstanding	*Included in cheque*
£	
13.99	✓
24.99	✓
71.02	✓
82.40	✓
17.95	
21.95	

Remittance Advice	
Account: M Pagan Ltd	
Outstanding	*Included in cheque*
£	
30.00	✓
35.00	✓
15.00	✓
40.00	✓
40.00	
25.00	

Internal report on receipts

Cheques and remittance advices received	Action

Sales ledger

A TATLOCK PLC

		£			£
1 April	Bal b/d	197.38	16 April	Bank	97.38
17 April	Sales	210.51	24 April	Bank	310.51
27 April	Sales	192.40			

P DAVIES PLC

		£			£
1 April	Bal b/d	-	17 April	Bank	194.30
3 April	Sales	294.30	21 April	Bank	151.37
14 April	Sales	151.37			
27 April	Sales	684.50			

Transactions for the Blackpool shop for April 20X7

			£
April	1	Balances	
		Cash in hand	21.90
		Bank (overdrawn)	101.45
	3	Cheques received/banked	1,016.94
	7	Cash sales	394.60
	8	Cash to bank	200.00
	13	Cheques received and banked	440.50
	18	Cash sales	264.66
	19	Cash to bank	300.00
	22	Cheques banked from debtors	760.00
	28	Cash to bank	100.00

Two column cash book

Date	Details	Cash £	Bank £	Date	Details	Cash £	Bank £
				2.4.X7	Sundry payments ★	11.50	2,165.83

★ This devolved assessment tests income and receipts, but payments are summarised so you can balance the cash book.

BPP PUBLISHING

TRIAL RUN DEVOLVED ASSESSMENT 2

FOUNDATION STAGE - NVQ/SVQ2

Unit 1

Recording Income and Receipts

The purpose of this Trial Run Devolved Assessment is to give you an idea of what an AAT simulation looks like. It is not intended as a definitive guide to the tasks you may be required to perform.

The suggested time allowance for this Assessment is **four hours,** two hours for part 1 and two hours for part 2. Up to 30 minutes extra time may be permitted in an AAT simulation. Breaks in assessment will be allowed in the AAT simulation, but it must normally be completed in one day.

Calculators may be used but no reference material is permitted.

**DO NOT OPEN THIS PAPER UNTIL YOU ARE READY TO START
UNDER TIMED CONDITIONS**

PART 1 - GROW EASY

INSTRUCTIONS

This Assessment is designed to test your ability to record income and receipts.

The situation is provided on Page 55.

You are provided with data on Pages 57 to 62 which you must use to complete the related tasks on Page 56.

Your answers should be set out on Pages 57 to 62 using the documents provided. You may require additional answer pages.

You are allowed two hours to complete your work.

A high level of accuracy is required. Check your work carefully.

Correcting fluid may be used but should be used in moderation. Errors should be crossed out neatly and clearly. You should write in black ink, not pencil.

You are advised to read the whole of the Assessment before commencing as all of the information may be of value and is not necessarily supplied in the sequence in which you might wish to deal with it.

A full answer to this Assessment is provided on Page 142 of this Kit.

THE SITUATION

Your name is Simon Dutton and you are the accounts clerk for a medium sized garden centre, Grow-Easy Ltd, 25 Parkside, Kendal LA9 7BL, in the north of England.

Today is Thursday 24 April 20X7.

The business

The company sells a variety of plants produced from the Grow-Easy Nursery and a range of garden tools, implements and garden ornaments. It has also started to make a small range of wooden garden furniture. Although some sales are credit sales the significant majority of the sales are for cash within the garden centre itself. The firm is below the compulsory registration limit for VAT and consequently has not registered.

Sales/income

All amounts received from cash and credit customers are banked at the end of each working day and one of your duties is to make out receipts for those customers who have asked for one and also to complete the daily analysis of payments received on the payments received analysis form.

There are four cash till points in the garden centre and at the end of each day all cash is removed and summarised, before banking, onto a cash reconciliation sheet. All the cash is banked with the exception of a £25 float (for each cash till) which is kept overnight in the garden centre safe. Each cash till requires an opening float for the following morning of:

1	£10 note
1	£5 note
5	£1 coins
2	50p coins
20	10p coins
20	5p coins
40	2p coins
20	1p coins

THE TASKS TO BE PERFORMED

		Blank document on page(s)
1	Make out a receipt for those customers who have requested one.	57-59
2	Complete the Payments Received Analysis Form for Thursday 24 April, including all credit customers, whether they require a receipt or not.	59
3	Complete the cash reconciliation sheet, prior to banking.	60
4	The cheques received today from credit customers are summarised in the data provided. You are required to complete the bank paying in slip.	61
5	The company's bank statement for the month ending 31 March is enclosed alongside details of the company's monthly standing orders. You are required to check the bank statements to ensure that all standing orders are correct and to explain what action you would taken in respect of any discrepancies.	63
6	The company's cash book for the month ended 31.3.X7 is provided. You are required to prepare a bank reconciliation statement as at 31.3.X7.	–

DATA

Receipts from customers

The following payments were received from customers, on Thursday 24 April 20X7, requiring a receipt

Payment from	Payment method	Amount £	Invoice number
Mr J Alexander	Cheque	341.72	B741
Ms C Hall	Cash	17.46	B726
Mr S Hill	Cash	23.40	B749
Mrs J Dawson	Cheque	14.36	B801
Mr M Wright	Cheque	101.26	B794
Mr I Clinton	Cheque	94.78	B797

The next receipt number is R202.

No _____	No _____ Grow-Easy _____ 20 ____
_____ 20 ____	Received from _____
From _____	the sum of _____ pounds _____ pence cheque/cash
£ _____	£ Signature _____

No _____	No _____ Grow-Easy _____ 20 ____
_____ 20 ____	Received from _____
From _____	the sum of _____ pounds _____ pence cheque/cash
£ _____	£ Signature _____

No _____

_____ 20 _____

From _____

£ _____

No _____   Grow-Easy _____ 20 _____

Received
from   _____

the sum of   _____ pounds
                                                  pence
              _____
                              cheque/cash

£   Signature   _____

No _____

_____ 20 _____

From _____

£ _____

No _____   Grow-Easy _____ 20 _____

Received
from   _____

the sum of   _____ pounds
                                                  pence
              _____
                              cheque/cash

£   Signature   _____

No _____

_____ 20 _____

From _____

£ _____

No _____   Grow-Easy _____ 20 _____

Received
from   _____

the sum of   _____ pounds
                                                  pence
              _____
                              cheque/cash

£   Signature   _____

No _____	No _____ Grow-Easy _____ 20 ____
_____ 20 ____	Received from _____
From _____	the sum of _____ pounds _____ pence
	cheque/cash
£ _____	£ _____ Signature _____

Payments received analysis form

Date	Customer	Amount £	Method Cash/cheque	Invoice Number
		═════		
		═════		

£

Totals: cash

cheque _____

═══════

BPP PUBLISHING

Closing cash balances in cash tills on 24 April 20X7 were as follows.

	Cash till number			
	1	*2*	*3*	*4*
£20 notes	2	3	1	1
£10 notes	4	6	2	5
£5 notes	2	2	1	3
£1 coins	10	18	4	9
50p coins	6	4	2	1
20p coins	40	21	10	11
10p coins	16	49	36	15
5p coins	21	40	30	8
2p coins	84	71	44	27
1p coins	70	60	39	68

Cash reconciliation sheet

	Notes					*Coins*				
	£20	*£10*	*£5*	*£1*	*50p*	*20p*	*10p*	*5p*	*2p*	*1p*
Cash till										
1										
2										
3										
4										
Total										
Less float required										
To be banked										
Number										
Value £										

Cheques received

Cheques received from credit customers on 24 April 20X7 were as follows.

	£	*Invoice number*
J Alexander	341.72	B741
P Phillips	79.46	B646
J Dawson	14.36	B801
M Wright	101.26	B794
S Lee	296.30	B793
S Churchward	27.37	B699
C Drury	74.90	B785
I Clinton	94.78	B797

Date _____

£50 notes	
£20 notes	
£10 notes	
£5 notes	
£1	
50p	
20p	
10p	
5p	
Bronze	
Total	
Cash	
Cheques (see over)	
£	

bank giro credit

Paid in by/Customer's Reference

Date _____

Code No: 40-70-68
Bank: Cumbria Bank PLC
Branch: Kendal

Credit: **GROW-EASY LTD**
Account No: 40711396

Number of Cheques

Paid in by _____

£50 notes	
£20 notes	
£10 notes	
£5 notes	
£1	
50p	
20p	
10p	
5p	
Bronze	
Total	
Cash	
Cheques (see over)	
£	

Cheque analysis			Counterfoil	
Name	Invoice No	£	Name	£

Bank statement

Cumbria Bank Plc			**CONFIDENTIAL**	

High Street
Kendal
Telephone   01542 111 2222

Account   Grow-Easy   SHEET NO   131

20X7   Statement date   19 March   Account no   40711396

Date	Details	Payments(£)	Receipts(£)	Balance (£)
1 March 20X7				256.06 OD
7 March 20X7		243.45		499.51 OD
9 March 20X7			1006.59	507.08
12 March 20X7	SO Electricity	79.00		428.08
18 March 20X7		1143.17		715.09 OD
18 March 20X7	SO Gas Board	95.00		810.09 OD
19 March 20X7			2391.74	1581.65
19 March 20X7		1107.93		473.72
20 March 20X7			1983.46	2457.18
22 March 20X7	SO BT	200.00		2257.18
25 March 20X7		179.47		2077.71
28 March 20X7			1741.26	3818.97

Key	**SO** Standing Order	**DV** Dividend	**CC** Cash &/or Cheques	**CGS** Charges	**PY** Payroll	**INT** Interest
	EC Eurocheque	**TR** Transfer	**CP** Card Purchases	**DD** Direct Debit	**OD** Overdrawn	**ADJ** Adjustment

Details of company standing orders

1   *Northern Electricity Board*. Direct debit payable on 12th of each month for £79.00.

2   *Northern Gas Board*. The annual payment of £1,260.00 is payable in 12 equal instalments on the 18th of each month.

3   *British Telecom* standing order of £2,400.00 for a full year divided into 12 equal instalments on the 22nd of each month.

Standing orders	Action

Cash book

CASH BOOK (MARCH 20X7)

	£		£
8.3.X7	1,006.59	1.3.X7 Balance b/d	256.06
17.3.X7	2,391.74	5.3.X7	243.45
19.3.X7	1,983.46	16.3.X7	1,143.17
26.3.X7	1,741.26	17.3.X7	1,107.93
30.3.X7	596.40	23.3.X7	179.47
		31.3.X7	894.72
		31.3.X7 Balance c/d	3,894.65
	7,719.45		7,719.45

PART 2: WORKBASE OFFICE SUPPLIES

INSTRUCTIONS

This Assessment is designed to test your ability to record income and receipts.

The situation is provided on Page 65.

You are provided with data on Pages 66 – 78 which you must use to complete the related tasks on Pages 66 - 78.

Your answers should be set out on Pages 66 - 78 using the documents provided. You may require additional answer pages.

You are allowed two hours to complete your work.

A high level of accuracy is required. Check your work carefully.

Correcting fluid may be used but should be used in moderation. Errors should be crossed out neatly and clearly. You should write in black ink, not pencil.

You are advised to read the whole of the Assessment before commencing as all of the information may be of value and is not necessarily supplied in the sequence in which you might wish to deal with it.

A full answer to this Assessment is provided on Page 148 of this Kit.

THE SITUATION

Your employer is Workbase Office Supplies Ltd ('Workbase'), a supplier of office equipment, mainly to business customers, with a single sales office based in Liverpool.

All sales invoices and credit notes are recorded in the sales day book. There is no separate sales returns day book.

You work in a department running the sales ledger. Your duties include preparation of invoices and credit notes by reference to supporting documentation (despatch notes, goods returned notes, both of which should be signed by the warehouse manager), customer details and the Workbase Office Supplies price list.

You are responsible for the maintenance of the sales day book, and the sales ledger. Note that any adjustments to the ledger accounts, other than those which derive from routine postings from the books of prime record, must be authorised in writing by the General Manager.

THE TASKS TO BE PERFORMED

TASK 1

The directors of Workbase have become concerned about the problem of slow payment of debts, which costs the company money because it must pay overdraft interest to the bank. The company decided to offer a settlement discount on all sales made from 1 August 20X5. The discount is 2% of the value of the goods (after any trade discount due has been deducted) for payment within 14 days of the invoice date.

Write a memo to Mr Denton, using the memo form below, explaining the VAT treatment which should be applied, now that settlement discounts are offered. Using an example, show how much VAT will be charged if a customer either (a) does or (b) does not take up the settlement discount.

WORKBASE OFFICE SUPPLIES LTD

MEMORANDUM

TASK 2

Mr Denton gives you a batch of three of today's invoices (see Pages 68 to 70) on which the goods total, net total and VAT figures have not yet been entered. The invoices may contain other errors, and maybe incomplete in other ways. However, the product codes and quantities have been agreed with despatch notes and are therefore known to be correct.

You are required to check the invoices, correcting where necessary. Product descriptions do not need to be exactly as shown in the catalogue, but they do need to be correct and to identify the product. Fill in any additional details necessary prior to the despatch of the invoices to customers.

Mr Denton also gives you a partially completed credit note (Page 71) for goods which Workbase has accepted as returns. The usual trade discount and the settlement discount of 2% were offered when the returned goods were originally invoiced. The original invoice was not paid. Complete the credit note for authorisation.

Note. You may need to refer to the Workbase Office Supplies Catalogue, price list and customer account details on Pages 72 to 75.

WORKBASE OFFICE SUPPLIES LTD

**63 Conduit Street
Liverpool L1 6NN**

Telephone: 0151-432 2222
Fax: 0151-432 2210

VAT Reg No. 924 4614 29

Invoice No. *894*

Account No.   *C011*

Date/Tax point *22 August 20X5*

Coals of Newcastle Ltd
25A Hive Street
Newcastle-upon-Tyne
NE4 6PR

Product code	Description	Quantity	Unit price £ p	Total amount £ p
F58110	Ambico 12-shelf unit	4	226.00	904.00
F10577	Ambience 9-drawer cabinet	2	484.50	969.00
A89811	Priory system tray sets (smoke)	6	14.27	114.16
			Goods total: less 10%: discount:	
Comments:			NET TOTAL VAT @ 17.5%	
2% settlement discount for payment within 14 days of invoice date			TOTAL	

Registered office: 63 Conduit Street, Liverpool L1 6NN   Registered No: 822 4742

WORKBASE OFFICE SUPPLIES LTD

**63 Conduit Street
Liverpool L1 6NN**

Telephone: 0151-432 2222
Fax: 0151-432 2210

VAT Reg No. 924 4614 29

Invoice No. *895*

Account No.　　*B020*

Date/Tax point *22 August 20X5*

Bowser & Bowser
22 Canard Lane
Duckley
SR1 1RF

Product code	Description	Quantity	Unit price £　p	Total amount £　p
G12352	Packs black med. Ultrapoint	50	6.08	304.00
G14000	Packs HB Office Star pencils	24	2.58	61.92
A22588	600F 4-hole fixed punch	20	20.47	409.40
G14384	Two colour Hi-Lite Jumbo marker	120	1.71	205.20
G14393	Fine red Hi-Lite Jumbo marker	30	0.94	28.20
			Goods total: less 10%: discount:	

Comments:	NET TOTAL	
2% settlement discount	VAT @ 17.5%	
for payment within 14 days of invoice date	TOTAL	

Registered office: 63 Conduit Street, Liverpool L1 6NN　　　　Registered No: 822 4742

WORKBASE OFFICE SUPPLIES LTD

63 Conduit Street
Liverpool L1 6NN

Invoice No. *896*

Telephone: 0151-432 2222
Fax: 0151-432 2210

VAT Reg No. 924 4614 29

Account No.   *U001*

Date/Tax point *22 August 20X5*

Underwood Dairies
Milk Street
Kingston
SR7 4NR

Product code	Description	Quantity	Unit price £ p	Total amount £ p
F71610	Chequers 472E chair (Oatmeal)	1	212.00	212.00
F74700	Exeter 420L chair (Fern)	2	296.00	296.00
F10420	Ambience multidrawer cabinets (Grey)	4	186.20	372.40
F55550	1200 workstation base unit	1	85.15	170.30
			Goods total: less 15% discount:	

Comments:

2% settlement discount

for payment within 14 days of invoice date

NET TOTAL	
VAT @ 17.5%	
TOTAL	

Registered office: 63 Conduit Street, Liverpool L1 6NN   Registered No: 822 4742

WORKBASE OFFICE SUPPLIES LTD

63 Conduit Street
Liverpool L1 6NN

Telephone: 0151-432 2222
Fax: 0151-432 2210

VAT Reg No. 924 4614 29

Credit Note No. *C451*

Account No.   *U001*

Date/Tax point   *22 August 20X5*

Underwood Dairies
Milk Street
Kingston
SR7 4NR

Product code	Description	Quantity	Unit price £ p	Total amount £ p
A87821	Tower 300 filing trays	10		
A87822	Tower 400 filing trays	15		

Comments:

Returned goods (original invoice no. 872)

NET TOTAL	
VAT @ 17.5%	
TOTAL	

Registered office: 63 Conduit Street, Liverpool L1 6NN   Registered No: 822 4742

Workbase office Supplies Limited
Quality products for your office environment

Catalogue and price list

[Extracts from the catalogue are set out below]

Code no

OFFICE FURNITURE

Exeter 420L Executive chair

Oatmeal	F74700
Fern	F74710
Charcoal	F74720

Chequers 472E Conference chair

Oatmeal	F76400
Charcoal	F76410

Chequers 474E Typist's chair

Paprika	F71600
Oatmeal	F71610
Fern	F71620
Charcoal	F71630

Ambience multidrawer filing cabinets

Grey	F10420
Coffee/cream	F10430

Ambience card filing cabinet

For 6" × 4" cards (9 drawers) - grey	F10577
For 8" × 5" cards (7 drawers) - grey	F10579

Stakkaform shelving units

These units offer a combined filing and working area for computer operators. Available in two sizes, the top and base units may be purchased together or the base unit may be purchased separately.

600 workstation top and base unit	F55540
600 workstation base unit	F55550
1200 workstation top and base unit	F55640
1200 workstation base unit	F55650

Ambico shelving

Steel posts and polyester-coated steel shelves, adjustable at 1" intervals

6-shelf unit	F58110
12-shelf unit	F58120
18-shelf unit	F58130

Code no

OFFICE ACCESSORIES

Tara file trolleys

Available in three sizes. Trays not included

Holds 6 'Tower 300' filing trays	A87724
Holds 12 'Tower 300' filing trays	A87725
Holds 6 'Tower 400' filing trays	A87726

Tara filing trays

Tower 300	A87821
Tower 400	A87822

Prior System 3 triple tier tray sets

Smoke	A89810
Grey	A89811
Slate blue	A89812

Perfex punches and perforators

420 heavy duty perforator. Two-hole, 8cm gauge	A22410
340 medium duty perforator. Two-hole, 8cm gauge	A22421
120 mini-punch. Capacity: 8 sheets	A22500
600F 4-hole fixed punch	A22588

PENS, PENCILS AND MARKERS

Ultrapoint ball pens

Fine point. Black. Pack of 50	G12342
Fine point. Blue. Pack of 50	G12343
Fine point. Red. Pack of 50	G12344
Fine point. Green. Pack of 12	G12345
Medium point. Black. Pack of 50	G12352
Medium point. Blue. Pack of 50	G12353
Medium point. Red. Pack of 50	G12354
Medium point. Green. Pack of 12	G12355

HI-life Jumbo markers

Chisel point. Black	G14385
Chisel point. Red	G14386
Fine point. Black	G14392
Fine point. Red	G14393
Two-colour marker. Black and red	G14384

Office Star pencils. The popular general office pencil

Supplied in packs of 12

4B	G14001
HB	G14000
3H	G14002
B	G14003
2H	G14004

Workbase Office Supplies Limited

Price list

Prices exclude VAT • Please use the product codes shown • Products are supplied singly unless otherwise stated • All goods are carriage paid

The prices of items listed in the catalogue extracts are set out below

Code no	Price £	Code no	Price £
A22410	23.45	G14000	2.58
A22421	10.92	G14001	2.58
A22500	1.64	G14002	2.58
A22588	20.47	G14003	2.58
A87724	65.00	G14004	2.58
A87725	94.00	G14384	1.71
A87726	82.00	G14385	1.21
A87821	4.92	G14386	1.21
A87822	6.13	G14392	0.94
A89810	14.27	G14393	0.94
A89811	14.27		
A89812	14.27		
F10420	186.20		
F10430	186.20		
F10577	484.50		
F10579	464.00		
F55540	189.90		
F55550	85.15		
F55640	276.50		
F55650	104.25		
F58110	126.00		
F58120	226.00		
F58130	338.00		
F71600	136.00		
F71610	136.00		
F71620	136.00		
F71630	136.00		
F74700	296.00		
F74710	296.00		
F74720	296.00		
F76400	212.00		
F76410	212.00		
G12342	6.08		
G12343	6.08		
G12344	6.08		
G12345	1.45		
G12352	6.08		
G12353	6.08		
G12354	6.08		
G12355	1.45		

Workbase Office Supplies Limited

List of customer discounts and credit limits: August 20X5
For internal use only

	Account no	% Discount	Credit limit £
Rabbit Fast Food Franchises Ltd	R001	25	500
Bowser & Bowser	B020	25	1,500
Roundabout Supplies Ltd	R002	20	500
Underwood Dairies	U001	20	500
Brittan's Farm Management Ltd	B007	20	500
Keats & Joyce	K010	15	1,000
Rank & Co	R005	15	750
Conduit Insurance Co plc	C002	15	500
John Cotton (Grantley) Ltd	C008	10	500
Whiterock Publishing Ltd	W011	10	500
Fawsley's & Co Ltd	F003	10	2,000
Coals of Newcastle Ltd	C011	10	2,000

All credit customers not on the above list are entitled to a 10% discount on the full value of orders over £100.

Workbase Office Supplies Limited

Nominal ledger account codes

Sales ledger control	2000
Purchase ledger control	3000
VAT control	3500
Sales A	5710
Sales F	5720
Sales G	5730
Sales sundry	5790
Bad debts expense	6350

TASK 3

Record the items you have dealt with in Tasks 1 and 2 in the sales day book below, classifying sales according to the initial letter of the product code. Total the sales day book.

Enter the necessary postings for these items to the general ledger and the debtors ledger on the ledger postings form given on Page 77.

WORKBASE OFFICE SUPPLIES LTD

SALES DAY BOOK

Date	Invoice/CN No.	Customer No.	Total	A	F	G	Sundry Sales	VAT

WORKBASE OFFICE SUPPLIES LTD

no 801

Ledger Postings

Date of transactions:　22 August 20X5

Account name	Account code	NOMINAL LEDGER		MEMORANDUM ACCOUNTS	
		DR £　p	CR £　p	DR £　p	CR £　p
Totals					

Authorised by _____　date _____

Posted by _____　date _____

BPP PUBLISHING

TASK 4

Prepare a further ledger postings form below for the following two items.

(a) The write-off of the balance of £321.70 on Meadwaite Ltd's account (code M070) as this is a bad debt which is now nine months old

(b) A contra entry to set off the balance of £94.00 on Spooner Ltd's purchase ledger account (code 801S) against the same company's sales ledger account (code S700).

WORKBASE OFFICE SUPPLIES LTD   no 802

Ledger Postings

Date of transactions:

Account name	Account code	NOMINAL LEDGER		MEMORANDUM ACCOUNTS	
		DR £ p	CR £ p	DR £ p	CR £ p
Totals					

Authorised by _____ date _____

Posted by _____ date _____

TRIAL RUN DEVOLVED ASSESSMENT 3

FOUNDATION STAGE - NVQ/SVQ2

Unit 1

Recording Income and Receipts

The purpose of this Trial Run Devolved Assessment is to give you an idea of what an AAT simulation looks like. It is not intended as a definitive guide to the tasks you may be required to perform.

The suggested time allowance for this Assessment is **four hours,** two hours for part 1 and two hours for part 2. Up to 30 minutes extra time may be permitted in an AAT simulation. Breaks in assessment will be allowed in the AAT simulation, but it must normally be completed in one day.

Calculators may be used but no reference material is permitted.

**DO NOT OPEN THIS PAPER UNTIL YOU ARE READY TO START
UNDER TIMED CONDITIONS**

PART 1: PAPER PRODUCTS

INSTRUCTIONS

This Assessment is designed to test your ability to record and account for cash transactions.

The situation is provided on Page 81.

You are provided with data on Pages 83 to 99 which you must use to complete the related tasks on Page 82.

Your answers should be set out on Pages 88 to 99 using the documents provided. You may require additional answer pages.

You are allowed two hours to complete your work.

A high level of accuracy is required. Check your work carefully.

Correcting fluid may be used but should be used in moderation. Errors should be crossed out neatly and clearly. You should write in black ink, not pencil.

You are advised to read the whole of the Assessment before commencing as all of the information may be of value and is not necessarily supplied in the sequence in which you might wish to deal with it.

A full answer to this Assessment is provided on Page 158 of this Kit.

THE SITUATION

Your name is Alison Greenwood and you are the bookkeeper for Paper Products Ltd, 139 Garstang Road, Preston PR1 8HG.

It is Friday 30 May 20X7.

The business is a wholesaler and mail order supplier of stationery products. It now sells a wide variety of stationery products by mail order and to stationery suppliers and retailers and has a sales team which covers the whole country.

The business is registered for Value Added Tax.

Your duties as bookkeeper include the following.

(a)   Checking sales invoices prior to their despatch to clients, by reference to customer details and your suppliers price list.

(b)   Occasionally preparing sales invoices from despatch notes.

(c)   Preparing, as necessary, credit notes for customers.

(d)   Entering data into the appropriate day books.

(e)   Posting invoices to the relevant memorandum sales accounts.

(f)   Completing the nominal ledger accounts.

BPP
PUBLISHING

THE TASKS TO BE PERFORMED

		Blank documents on page(s)
1	Check the sales invoices about to be sent out on Pages 85-87 and if you are not satisfied indicate, on the form provided, what action you would take. The next invoice number is 2507.	88
2	Refer to the despatch notes and prepare sales invoices using the blank invoice forms.	91-93
3	Prepare the necessary credit notes that have been authorised. The next credit note number is 117.	94
4	Enter all the approved sales invoices and credit notes into the sales day book and the sales returns day book. Assume that any sales invoices which needed correction have now been corrected.	95-96
5	Post the invoices and credit notes, for 30 May 20X7, to the memorandum sales ledger accounts.	97-98
6	Complete the sales ledger control and VAT control accounts and the general (nominal) ledger sales accounts.	98-99

Note. VAT should be rounded up or down to the nearest penny.

DATA

Customer details

Name	Address	Trade discount %
Alexander Ltd	201 Blackburn Road Bolton BL1 2HE	10
Consumer Products Ltd	105 Coventry Road Walsall B12 OEP	5
Halton Group Ltd	94 Edinburgh Way Dundee DD10 OPR	10
Ronald Davies Distribution	Ronald Davies House 10 Argyll Street Plymouth PL2 5BC	10
Stationery Stores Ltd	16 Greenbank Road Ipswich IP32 4QD	7.5
Clinton and Wright Distribution Ltd	201 Eastgate Road Bristol BS1 2HE	10

BPP PUBLISHING

Extracts from Paper Products Ltd Suppliers Price list

Code	Product	Price (exc VAT £)
	Computer disk box	
604	- Per 10	19.50
606	- Per 100	180.00
602	- Single	2.25
	Computer paper	
612	- 1,000 (sheets)	18.45
617	- 2,000 (sheets)	34.70
629	Labels (5,000 box)	17.50
	Box files(10)	
635	- A4	12.50
646	- Foolscap	13.90
	A4 Ring binder (10)	
652	- Black	26.20
653	- Blue	26.40
654	- Other colours	28.10
	Lever Arch file (10)	
659	- A4	13.10
671	- Foolscap	14.40
	Paperclips (1,000)	
675	- Large	2.20
676	- Small	1.80
	Roller ball pen (10)	
678	- Black	8.40
679	- Blue	8.60
680	- Red	8.80
681	- Green	8.90
	Highlighter (12)	
694	- Yellow	10.50
695	- Green	10.50
696	- Pink	10.20
	Memo pads (12)	
703	- A4	17.40
707	- Foolscap	19.60
	Envelopes (100)	
710	- White (small)	7.80
712	- White (large)	11.40
714	- Ivory (small)	9.20
716	- Ivory (large)	13.70
	Magnetic markers	
720	- 15mm - per 100	54.00
721	- 15mm - per 200	98.00
722	- 25mm - per 100	71.50
723	- 25mm - per 200	126.80

PAPER PRODUCTS LTD

139 Garstang Road, Preston PR1 8HG
Tel: 01772 604007   Fax: 01772 604931

SALES INVOICE

VAT No.: 220 5564 12

Invoice No.   2507

Date/Tax point: 30.5.X7

Item Description	Code	Quantity	Unit price	Total
			£ p	£ p
A4 Ring binders - black	652	5 packs of 10	26.20	131.00
Paperclips - large	675	7 boxes	2.20	15.40
Envelopes - white - large	712	8 packs	11.40	91.20

Total	237.60
Trade discount (%) -10%	(23.76)
Net	213.84
VAT @ 17.5%	37.42
Amount due	251.26

To: Alexander Ltd
       201 Blackburn Road
       Bolton
       BL1 2HE

PAPER PRODUCTS LTD

139 Garstang Road, Preston PR1 8HG

Tel: 01772 604007   Fax: 01772 604931

SALES INVOICE   Invoice No.   2508

VAT No.: 220 5564 12   Date/Tax point: 30.5.X7

Item Description	Code	Quantity	Unit price	Total
			£ p	£ p
Computer paper	612	6 boxes of 1000 sheets	18.45	110.70
Labels	629	3 boxes of 5000	19.50	58.50
Memo pads	703	7 packs of 12	17.40	121.80
Magnetic markers (15mm)	720	3 boxes of 100	54.00	162.00

Total	453.00
Trade discount (%) -10%	(45.30)
Net	407.70
VAT @ 17.5%	71.35
Amount due	479.05

To: Halton Group Ltd
      94 Edinburgh Way
      Dundee
      DD10 0PR

PAPER PRODUCTS LTD

139 Garstang Road, Preston PR1 8HG

Tel: 01772 604007   Fax: 01772 604931

SALES INVOICE

VAT No.: 220 5564 12

			Invoice No.	2509
			Date/Tax point:	30.5.X7

Item Description	Code	Quantity	Unit price	Total
			£ p	£ p
A4 - Ring binders - Black	652	5 boxes of 10	26.20	131.00
- Blue	653	7 boxes of 10	26.40	184.80
Lever arch file - foolscap	671	4 boxes of 10	14.40	57.60
Memo pads - A4	703	12 boxes of 12	17.40	208.80
Envelopes - ivory - small	714	3 boxes of 100	9.20	27.60

Total	609.80
Trade discount (%) -10%	(60.98)
Net	548.82
VAT @ 17.5%	106.72
Amount due	655.54

To: Ronald Davies Distribution
      Ronald Davies House
      10 Argyll Street
      Plymouth PL2 5BC

BPP PUBLISHING

Sales invoice check - invoice number	Action

PAPER PRODUCTS LTD

139 Garstang Road, Preston PR1 8HG
Tel: 01772 604007   Fax: 01772 604931

DESPATCH NOTE

TO: Consumer Products Ltd
      105 Coventry Road
      Walsall B12 0EP

We would like to advise you that the following goods have been despatched

CODE NO	DESCRIPTION	QUANTITY
604	Disc boxes	2
617	Computer paper	5
696	Highlighters	10
703	Memo pads	4

PAPER PRODUCTS LTD

139 Garstang Road, Preston PR1 8HG
Tel: 01772 604007   Fax: 01772 604931

DESPATCH NOTE

TO: Stationery Stores Ltd
      16 Greenbank Road
      Ipswich IP32 4QD

We would like to advise you that the following goods have been despatched

CODE NO	DESCRIPTION	QUANTITY
629	Labels	8
652	Ring binders	3
676	Papers clips	14
681	Pens	5

BPP PUBLISHING

PAPER PRODUCTS LTD

139 Garstang Road, Preston PR1 8HG
Tel: 01772 604007   Fax: 01772 604931

DESPATCH NOTE

TO: Clinton and Wright Distribution Ltd
      201 Eastgate Road
      Bristol BA1 2HD

We would like to advise you that the following goods have been despatched

CODE NO	DESCRIPTION	QUANTITY
612	Computer paper	4
629	Labels	6
654	Ring binders	2
694	Highlighters	9

Sales invoices

PAPER PRODUCTS LTD

139 Garstang Road, Preston PR1 8HG

Tel: 01772 604007   Fax: 01772 604931

SALES INVOICE			Invoice No.	
VAT No.: 220 5564 12			Date/Tax point:	

Item Description	Code	Quantity	Unit price	Total
			£ p	£ p

Total	
Trade discount (%)	
Net	
VAT @ 17.5%	
Amount due	

To:

PAPER PRODUCTS LTD

139 Garstang Road, Preston PR1 8HG

Tel: 01772 604007   Fax: 01772 604931

SALES INVOICE

Invoice No.

VAT No.: 220 5564 12

Date/Tax point:

Item Description	Code	Quantity	Unit price		Total	
			£	p	£	p

Total	
Trade discount (%)	
Net	
VAT @ 17.5%	
Amount due	

To:

PAPER PRODUCTS LTD

139 Garstang Road, Preston PR1 8HG
Tel: 01772 604007   Fax: 01772 604931

SALES INVOICE   Invoice No.

VAT No.: 220 5564 12   Date/Tax point:

Item Description	Code	Quantity	Unit price		Total	
			£	p	£	p

Total
Trade discount (%)

Net
VAT @ 17.5%

Amount due

To:

Credit notes authorised to be issued

Organisation	*Details*
Alexander Ltd	Product 604: faulty - 1 box of 10 Product 694: 1 box short on delivery
Stationery Stores Ltd	Product 681: 2 boxes short on delivery

PAPER PRODUCTS LTD

139 Garstang Road, Preston PR1 8HG
Tel: 01772 604007   Fax: 01772 604931

CREDIT NOTE TO:

CREDIT NOTE

Vat reg:
Date/tax point:
Credit note no:

ITEM DESCRIPTION	CODE	QUANTITY	UNIT PRICE	TOTAL
Total				
Trade discount (%)				
Net				
VAT at 17.5%				
Total credit				

PAPER PRODUCTS LTD

139 Garstang Road, Preston PR1 8HG
Tel: 01772 604007   Fax: 01772 604931

CREDIT NOTE TO:

CREDIT NOTE

Vat reg:
Date/tax point:
Credit note no:

ITEM DESCRIPTION	CODE	QUANTITY	UNIT PRICE	TOTAL
Total				
Trade discount (%)				
Net				
VAT at 17.5%				
Total credit				

SALES DAY BOOK

**PAPER PRODUCTS LIMITED
SALES DAY BOOK**

Date	Invoice	Customer	Total £	VAT £	Boxes/binders/ files £	Paperclips/ labels £	Envelopes/ paper/pads £	Maker pens/ highlighters £
29.5.X7 b/d		Alexander	224.42	33.42	106.00	25.00	40.00	20.00
		Consumer Products	227.54	33.89	25.90	131.15	19.20	17.40
		Halton Group	72.38	10.78	-	-	12.00	49.60
		Ronald Davies	147.87	22.02	17.60	-	-	108.25
		Stationery Stores	100.58	14.98	36.20	49.40	-	-
		Clinton & Wright	94.94	14.14	29.00	17.00	-	34.80
30.5.X7								

SALES RETURNS DAY BOOK

Date	Credit note	Customer	Total £	VAT £	Boxes/binders/ files £	Paperclips/ labels £	Envelopes/ paper/pads £	Maker pens/ highlighters £
29.5.X7 b/d								

SALES LEDGER

ACCOUNT: ALEXANDER LTD					
Date	*Details*	*£*	*Date*	*Details*	*£*
29.5.X7	b/d	224.42			

ACCOUNT: HALTON GROUP LTD					
Date	*Details*	*£*	*Date*	*Details*	*£*
29.5.X7	b/d	72.38			

ACCOUNT: RONALD DAVIES DISTRIBUTION					
Date	*Details*	*£*	*Date*	*Details*	*£*
29.5.X7	b/d	147.87			

ACCOUNT: CONSUMER PRODUCTS LTD					
Date	*Details*	*£*	*Date*	*Details*	*£*
29.5.X7	b/d	227.54			

ACCOUNT: STATIONERY STORES LTD					
Date	*Details*	*£*	*Date*	*Details*	*£*
29.5.X7	b/d	100.58			

ACCOUNT: CLINTON AND WRIGHT LTD					
Date	*Details*	*£*	*Date*	*Details*	*£*
29.5.X7	b/d	94.94			

NOMINAL (GENERAL) LEDGER

ACCOUNT: SALES LEDGER CONTROL					
Date	*Details*	*£*	*Date*	*Details*	*£*
29.5.X7	b/d	867.73			

ACCOUNT: VAT CONTROL					
Date	*Details*	*£*	*Date*	*Details*	*£*
			29.5.X7	b/d	129.23

ACCOUNT: SALES - BOXES, BINDERS, FILES					
Date	Details	£	Date	Details	£
			29.5.X7	b/d	214.70

ACCOUNT: SALES - PAPERCLIPS, LABELS					
Date	Details	£	Date	Details	£
			29.5.X7	b/d	222.55

ACCOUNT: SALES - ENVELOPES, PAPER, PADS					
Date	Details	£	Date	Details	£
			29.5.X7	b/d	71.20

ACCOUNT: SALES - PENS, MARKERS, HIGHLIGHERS					
Date	Details	£	Date	Details	£
			29.5.X7	b/d	230.05

BPP PUBLISHING

PART 2: CATERING CONTRACTS

INSTRUCTIONS

This Assessment is designed to test your ability to record and account for credit transactions.

The situation is provided on Page 101.

You are provided with data on Pages 103-109 which you must use to complete the related tasks on Page 102.

Your answers should be set out on Pages 104-109 using the documents provided. You may require additional answer pages.

You are allowed four hours to complete your work.

A high level of accuracy is required. Check your work carefully.

Correcting fluid may be used but should be used in moderation. Errors should be crossed out neatly and clearly. You should write in black ink, not pencil.

You are advised to read the whole of the Assessment before commencing as all of the information may be of value and is not necessarily supplied in the sequence in which you might wish to deal with it.

A full answer to this Assessment is provided on Page 168 of this Kit.

THE SITUATION

Your name is Derek Oldfield and you are employed as the bookkeeper for Catering Contacts Ltd, an organisation which specialises in the supply of catering equipment to the catering industry.

The address of Catering Contacts Ltd is 75, Parr Street, Kendal, Cumbria LA9 5HE and today's date is Friday 27th June 20X7.

The business is registered for Value Added Tax and its products are bought and sold at a standard rate of 17.5%.

Your duties as bookkeeper include the following.

(a)   Entering sales invoices and credit notes into the sales day book and sales returns day book. Calculating invoice totals on a calculation sheet.

(b)   Posting individual transactions to customer's accounts in the sales ledger.

(c)   Posting day book totals to the relevant accounts in the general ledger.

(d)   Posting totals to the debtors control account.

THE TASKS TO BE PERFORMED

**Blank document
on page(s)**

Note. VAT should be rounded up or down to the nearest penny.

DATA

Invoice details

Note. Prices are before applying a discount.

Name	Details (excluding VAT)
Highland Hotels (23 June)	2 cookers at £195.99 each 36 utensils at £14.50 each 16 cutlery sets at £34.00 each
Happy Eaters Group (23 June)	8 cutlery sets at £34.00 each 1 hod at £297.60
Catering Consumables (24 June)	6 pans at £7.49 each 2 pans at £9.99 each
Sneddons Ltd (25 June)	11 pans at £9.99 each
Bensons Bakers Ltd (25 June)	1 oven hob at £157.80 3 cutlery sets at £34.00 each 17 baking trays at £2.75 each
Easy-Fry Co (25 June)	3 'chip pans' at £3.99 each 1 hob at £146.45 1 kettle at £17.40
Peak Manufacturing (26 June)	2 large pans at £42.75 each 11 kettles at £17.40 each 4 cutlery sets at £34.00 each 10 standard glasses at £1.49 each
Beautiful Bakers (27 June)	4 boxes of table mats at £8.90 each 15 small glasses at £1.29 each

Customer credit details and discounts available

Name	Discount %	Credit limit £
John Smith Ltd	15	4,800
Highland Hotels	25	17,000
Lakes Hotel Group	20	17,500
Fred's Fryer	15	2,500
Catering Consumables	10	6,500
Peak Manufacturing	20	7,000
Happy Eaters Group	10	11,000
Sneddon's Group	10	4,000
Easy-Fry Co	15	3,500
John's Snack Co	10	2,000

Customers not listed above are entitled to a minimum of 10% trade discount.

BPP PUBLISHING

INVOICE CALCULATION SHEET

Name	Details	Amount £	Less discount £	Net £	VAT £	Total £

SALES DAY BOOK

Date	Details	Invoice No	Goods £	VAT £	Total £

Details of credit notes needed

Happy Eaters Group

Overcharge on glasses: 72 glasses charged at £1.89 should have been £1.29 each.

Peak Manufacturing

Previous order supplied 6 cutlery sets at £34.00 rather than 8 sets invoiced.

SALES RETURNS DAY BOOK

Name	Details	Amount £	Less discount £	Net £	VAT £	Total £

SALES LEDGER

	£		£

	£		£

	£		£

	£		£

BPP PUBLISHING

	£		£

	£		£

	£		£

	£		£

GENERAL LEDGER

SALES ACCOUNT

£		£

VAT ACCOUNT

£		£

DEBTORS CONTROL ACCOUNT

£		£

BPP PUBLISHING

Answers to practice devolved assessments

ANSWER TO PRACTICE DEVOLVED ASSESSMENT 1: CONWAY

Tutorial note. This devolved assessment tests your ability to write up a cash book and perform a bank reconciliation. In practice, bank reconciliations will range from the straightforward to the very complex, usually depending on the volume of transactions passing through the account. You should also bear in mind that the principles of the bank reconciliation can be applied to many aspects of accounting, particularly where accounts in a company's books are compared with external statements or documents.

Answer

(a)   See Pages 114.

(b)   See Pages 115.

BPP
PUBLISHING

System XX4 BANK RECEIPTS 31 July 20X5

N/C Name: BANK CURRENT ACCOUNT
1000

Tax rate: 17.5%
Batch Total: 115,835.59

N/C DEP	DATE	CHEQUE DETAILS	Net amount	Tax amount	Gross amount
3420	0107X5	Fernlea (7)	2,960.88	0.00	2,960.88
7220	0107X5	M Parr	5,000.00	0.00	5,000.00
3450	0307X5	Levison (3)	1,284.74	0.00	1,284.74
3410	0407X5	Blackwood (10)	8,619.03	0.00	8,619.03
3460	0907X5	Elliot (1)	8,585.52	0.00	8,585.52
3430	0907X5	Portmans (6)	6,986.82	0.00	6,986.82
5580	1207X5	Inland Revenue	579.26	0.00	579.26
5800	1207X5	Sales Sundry	1,215.17	212.65	1,427.82
5520	1607X5	Electricity Board	61.70	10.80	72.50
7260	1907X5	Brokers Inc	3,247.92	0.00	3,247.92
5780	1907X5	Hunt Lodge	7,500.00	0.00	7,500.00
3460	2407X5	Elliot (2)	2,712.53	0.00	2,712.53
3440	2507X5	Banner-Crittel (4)	8,229.09	0.00	8,229.09
3430	2907X5	Portmans (7)	9,201.67	0.00	9,201.67
3410	2907X5	Blackwood (11)	31,572.84	0.00	31,572.84
3420	2907X5	Fernlea (8)	8,485.08	0.00	8,485.08
3450	3007X5	Levison (5)	6,898.69	0.00	6,898.69
3410	3007X5	Blackwood: excess	2,471.20	0.00	2,471.20
			115,612.14	223.45	115,835.59

JULY – RECEIPTS

	Date		Total	VAT	Sales Credit	Sales Sundry	Rent	Sundry	Fixed Assets
1	1 July	Brought forward	28,742 45						
2	1 July	Fernlea Manor (7)	2,960 88		2,960 88				
3	"	M Parr (car sold)	5,000 00						5,000 00
4	3 July	Levison House (3)	1,284 74		1,284 74				
5	4 July	Blackwood Park Estates (10)	8,619 03		8,619 03				
6	9 July	Elliot Grange (1)	8,585 52		8,585 52				
7	"	Portmans (6)	6,986 82		6,986 82				
8	12 July	Inland Revenue	579 26					579 26	
9	"	Public sale	1,427 82	212 65		1,215 17			
10	16 July	Electricity Board	72 50	10 80				61 70	
11	19 July	Brokers Inc. Sale of shares	3,247 92						3,247 92
12	"	Hunt Lodge rent	7,500 00				7,500 00		
13	24 July	Elliot Grange (2)	2,712 53		2,712 53				
14	25 July	Banner – Crittel (4)	8,229 09		8,229 09				
15	29 July	Portmans (7)	9,201 67		9,201 67				
16	"	Blackwood Park Estate (11)	31,572 84		31,572 84				
17	"	Fernlea Manor (8)	8,485 08		8,485 08				
18	30 July	Levison House (5)	6,898 69		6,898 69				
19	"	Blackwood Park Estates: excess	2,471 20		2,471 20		6,986 82		6,986 82
20									
21			144,578 04	223 45	98,008 09	1,215 17	7,500 00	640 96	8,247 92

(c)   BANK RECONCILIATION AS AT 31 JULY 20X5

	£	£
Balance per bank statement		(11,498.40)
Outstanding cheques		
January 4 110204	29.42	
July 12 113736	209.81	
July 19 113740	2,097.97	
July 25 113743	3,428.80	
July 25 113745	6,082.88	
July 26 113746	264.74	
July 26 113747	194.47	
July 30 113748	8,309.90	
July 30 113749	327.66	
		(20,945.65)
Outstanding lodgements		
July 29 Portmans	9,201.67	
July 29 Blackwood	31,572.84	
July 29 Fernlea	8,485.08	
July 30 Levison	6,898.69	
July 30 Blackwood	2,471.20	
		58,629.48
Bank errors		
Cheque 113729 debited twice	95.82	
Cheque 113742 debited twice	120.47	
		216.29
Corrected cash book balance		26,401.72
Cash book balance		27,332.22
Cash book omissions		
2 July bank charges not entered	448.21	
21 July DD Water	332.29	
27 July Unauthorised OD fee	150.00	
		(930.50)
		26,401.72

(d)   (i)   The cash book should be corrected for the following items.

   (1)   Cheque 110204 £29.42 should be written back to the cash book as it is now 'stale', being over six months old.

   (2)   £448.21 bank charges should be entered.

   (3)   £332.29 water rates direct debit should be entered.

   (4)   £150.00 overdraft fee should be entered.

   (ii)   The bank has entered cheques 113729 and 113742 twice on the bank statement. The bank should be asked to correct the bank statement during the following month.

   The company should also consider approaching the bank with a view to obtaining an overdraft facility. Although the company may be profitable, it will be necessary to finance working capital and any fixed asset investments as the company expands.

   A prearranged facility will avoid fees, such as that charged during July, when the company goes into overdraft. Obviously, the situation at the end of the month is more serious, although it appears that the bank are being cooperative and cheques are not yet being bounced.

ANSWER TO PRACTICE DEVOLVED ASSESSMENT 2: APPARAT

Tutorial note. The information set out below gives you enough information with which to check your answer, whether you are using a PC or manual processing.

Solution

(a)(b)(c)

St James Comprehensive School					Limit: £1,000
	Debit	£		*Credit*	£
4.6.X5	Balance	-			
6.6.X5	Invoice 1001	787.25			
25.6.X5	Invoice 1005	51.70	30.6.X5	Balance c/d	838.95
		838.95			838.95
1.7.X5	Balance b/f	838.95	3.7.X5	Payment	838.95
30.7.X5	Invoice 1013	105.75	31.7.X5	Balance c/d	105.75
		944.70			944.70
1.8.X5	Balance b/f	105.75	24.8.X5	Payment	105.75
8.8.X5	Invoice 1015	211.50			
22.8.X5	Invoice 1019	105.75	31.8.X5	Balance c/d	317.25
		423.00			423.00

Siward Ltd					Limit: £1,000
	Debit	£		*Credit*	£
4.6.X5	Balance	-			
8.6.X5	Invoice 1002	493.50	30.6.X5	Balance c/d	493.50
		493.50			493.50
1.7.X5	Balance b/f	493.50			
2.7.X5	Invoice 1007	246.75			
24.7.X5	Invoice 1010	928.25	31.7.X5	Balance c/d	1,668.50
		1,668.50			1,668.50
			27.8.X5	Payment	668.50
1.8.X5	Balance b/f	1,668.50	31.8.X5	Balance c/d	1,000.00
		1,688.50			1,688.50

Sedgedown Borough Council					Limit: £3,000
	Debit	£		*Credit*	£
4.6.X5	Balance	-			
28.6.X5	Invoice 1006	103.40	30.6.X5	Balance c/d	103.40
		103.40			103.40
1.7.X5	Balance b/f	103.40	25.7.X5	Payment	103.40
30.7.X5	Invoice 1012	2,937.50	31.7.X5	Balance c/d	2,937.50
		3,040.90			3,040.90
1.8.X5	Balance b/f	2,937.50	17.8.X5	Credit note 9003	587.50
27.8.X5	Invoice 1020	1,468.75	24.8.X5	Payment	2,350.00
2X.8.X5	Invoice 1021	282.00	31.8.X5	Balance c/d	1,750.75
		4,688.25			4,688.25

		Sada Ltd			Limit: £2,500
	Debit	£		*Credit*	£
4.6.X5	Balance	-	19.6.X5	Credit note 9001	411.25
14.6.X5	Invoice 1003	822.50	30.6.X5	Balance c/d	411.25
		822.50			822.50
1.7.X5	Balance b/f	411.25	26.7.X5	Payment	411.25
11.7.X5	Invoice 1008	411.25	31.7.X5	Balance c/d	411.25
		822.50			822.50
1.8.X5	Balance b/f	411.25			
15.8.X5	Invoice 1017	176.25			
20.8.X5	Invoice 1018	117.50	31.8.X5	Balance c/d	705.00
		705.00			705.00

		Graham Light (Projects) Ltd			Limit: £1,000
	Debit	£		*Credit*	£
4.6.X5	Balance	-			
18.6.X5	Invoice 1004	822.50	30.6.X5	Balance c/d	822.50
		822.50			822.50
1.7.X5	Balance b/f	822.50	31.7.X5	Balance c/d	822.50
		822.50			822.50
1.8.X5	Balance c/d	822.50			
29.8.X5	Invoice 1022	30.55	31.8.X5	Balance c/d	853.05
		853.05			853.05

		Babbage & Lovelace			Limit: £500
	Debit	£		*Credit*	£
4.6.X5	Balance	-			
18.7.X5	Invoice 1009	634.50	23.7.X5	Credit note 9002	634.50
27.7.X5	Invoice 1011	634.50			
30.7.X5	Invoice 1014	105.75	31.7.X5	Balance c/d	740.25
		1,374.75			1,374.75
1.8.X5	Balance b/f	740.25	2.8.X5	Payment	300.00
9.8.X5	Invoice 1016	58.75	31.8.X5	Balance c/d	499.00
		799.00			799.00

(d) *Customer statements of account as at 31 August 20X5*

STATEMENT OF ACCOUNT

Apparat Ltd, 7A Meadsway, Sedgedown SD1 2ND. Tel/Fax: 01664-24274
VAT Reg No: 01 424 4288
Customer name: St James Comprehensive School
Address: Kirk Avenue
        Sedgedown SD1 7PP   Date of statement: 31 August 20X5

Date	Description/reference	Debit £ p	Credit £ p	Balance £ p
30.7.X5	Invoice 1013	105.75		105.75
8.8.X5	Invoice 1015	211.50		317.25
22.8.X5	Invoice 1019	105.75		423.00
24.8.X5	Payment - thank you		105.75	317.25

AMOUNT NOW DUE	£317.25

Registered Office: 7A Meadsway, Sedgedown, SD1 2ND. Reg No. 18018047

STATEMENT OF ACCOUNT

Apparat Ltd, 7A Meadsway, Sedgedown SD1 2ND. Tel/Fax: 01664-24274
VAT Reg No: 01 424 4288
Customer name: Siward Ltd
Address: 39 Telford Way
        Ocset SD3 9DA
                                       Date of statement: 31 August 20X5

Date	Description/reference	Debit £ p	Credit £ p	Balance £ p
8.6.X5	Invoice 1002	493.50		493.50
2.7.X5	Invoice 1007	246.75		740.25
24.7.X5	Invoice 1010	928.25		1668.50
27.8.X5	Payment - thank you		668.50	1000.00

AMOUNT NOW DUE	£1000.00

Registered Office: 7A Meadsway, Sedgedown, SD1 2ND. Reg No. 18018047

STATEMENT OF ACCOUNT

Apparat Ltd, 7A Meadsway, Sedgedown SD1 2ND. Tel/Fax: 01664-24274
VAT Reg No: 01 424 4288
Customer name: Sedgedown Borough Council
Address: Education Department
      24 Meadsway
      Sedgedown SD1 2NE   Date of statement: 31 August 20X5

Date	Description/reference	Debit £ p	Credit £ p	Balance £ p
30.7.X5	Invoice 1012	2937.50		2937.50
17.8.X5	Credit note 9003		587.50	2350.00
24.8.X5	Payment - thank you		2350.00	
27.8.X5	Invoice 1020	1468.75		1468.75
29.8.X5	Invoice 1021	282.00		1750.75
AMOUNT NOW DUE				£1750.75

Registered Office: 7A Meadsway, Sedgedown, SD1 2ND. Reg No. 18018047

STATEMENT OF ACCOUNT

Apparat Ltd, 7A Meadsway, Sedgedown SD1 2ND. Tel/Fax: 01664-24274
VAT Reg No: 01 424 4288
Customer name: Sada Ltd
Address: Unit 33 Sedgedown Business Park
      Trowse Way
      Sedgedown SD2 1PA   Date of statement: 31 August 20X5

Date	Description/reference	Debit £ p	Credit £ p	Balance £ p
11.7.X5	Invoice 1008	411.25		411.25
15.8.X5	Invoice 1017	176.25		587.50
20.8.X5	Invoice 1018	117.50		705.00
AMOUNT NOW DUE				£705.00

Registered Office: 7A Meadsway, Sedgedown, SD1 2ND. Reg No. 18018047

STATEMENT OF ACCOUNT

Apparat Ltd, 7A Meadsway, Sedgedown SD1 2ND. Tel/Fax: 01664-24274
VAT Reg No: 01 424 4288
Customer name: Graham Light (Projects) Ltd
Address: 24A High Street
     Ribben Village
     Sedgedown SD7 4NO   Date of statement: 31 August 20X5

Date	Description/reference	Debit £ p	Credit £ p	Balance £ p
18.6.X5	Invoice 1004	822.50		822.50
29.8.X5	Invoice 1022	30.55		853.05
AMOUNT NOW DUE				£853.05

Registered Office: 7A Meadsway, Sedgedown, SD1 2ND. Reg No. 18018047

STATEMENT OF ACCOUNT

Apparat Ltd, 7A Meadsway, Sedgedown SD1 2ND. Tel/Fax: 01664-24274
VAT Reg No: 01 424 4288
Customer name: Babbage and Lovelace
Address: 2 Telford Way
     Ocset SD3 9DA   Date of statement: 31 August 20X5

Date	Description/reference	Debit £ p	Credit £ p	Balance £ p
27.7.X5	Invoice 1011	634.50		634.50
30.7.X5	Invoice 1014	105.75		740.25
2.8.X5	Payment - thank you		300.00	440.25
9.8.X5	Invoice 1016	58.75		499.00
AMOUNT NOW DUE				£499.00

Registered Office: 7A Meadsway, Sedgedown, SD1 2ND. Reg No. 18018047

(e)   *Apparat Ltd: Aged debtors' listing as at 31 August 20X5*

	Credit limit £	Total balance £	Up to 1 month £	2 months £	3 months £
St James Comp School	1,000	317.25	317.25		
Siward Ltd	1,000	1,000.00		1,000.00	
Sedgedown BC	3,000	1,750.75	1,750.75		
Sada Ltd	2,500	705.00	293.75	411.25	
Graham Light (P) Ltd	1,000	853.05	30.55		822.50
Babbage & Lovelace	500	499.00	58.75	440.25	
Total		5,125.05	2,451.05	1,851.50	822.50
Percentage		100.0	47.8	36.1	16.1

(f)   **Tutorial note**. Judgement is necessary in deciding what action to take on overdue debts. You may have reached valid conclusions which are a little different from ours. It *is* important that your conclusions are clear, and properly explained.

Memorandum

To: J R
From   A N Assistant   3 September 20X5

Subject: Debtors

An aged analysis of debtors as at 31 August 20X5 is attached [(see (e) above].

£2,674 (52.2%) of the total debt of £5,125 was overdue as at 31 August. All accounts were within credit limits at that date, but limits were exceeded on some accounts prior to this.

Of the six credit customers, all but two have overdue debts. The two customers which do not, St James and Sedgedown BC, have paid all of their debts on time so far, and have not exceeded their credit limits.

Siward has part-paid its July invoices to bring its balance down to £1,000. I recommend that no more credit sales should be made until the July balance is paid in full. In any case, Siward's balance is utilising its credit limit in full. A letter should be sent to the company. We should ensure that we do not make sales above the level of the credit limit again, as we have to Siward in the past.

Sada has not yet paid its July invoice for £411. The company paid its June balance on 26 July: it may be that an end-of-August payment is on its way to us. We should telephone the company to check this and to remind them that payment is due. Sada has not exceeded its credit limit.

Graham Light has made two purchases only, and no payment has yet been received. £822.50, the bulk of the balance, was invoiced on 18 June. A strongly worded letter is warranted.

£440, the bulk of Babbage & Lovelace's balance, comprises part of July invoices. The only payment made by the debtor so far has been a round sum of £300 on 2 August, suggesting that the debtor could be in financial difficulties. A reminder letter should be sent initially.

(g)

Letter to Siward

**Apparat Limited
7A Meadsway
Sedgedown
SD1 2ND**

Finance Director
Siward Ltd
3X Telford Way
Ocset SD3 9DA   3 September 20X5

Dear Sir (Madam)

I write to remind you that your balance of £1,000.00 with us now exceeds the 30-day period of credit allowed.

I look forward to receiving immediate payment of this amount.

Yours faithfully

Jill Regan
Managing Director

Note. The finance director should be addressed by name, if known. It may be tactful (and useful) to find out the name (and thereby the gender) of the finance director.

Letter to Graham Light

**Apparat Limited
7A Meadsway
Sedgedown
SD1 2ND**

Finance Director
Graham Light (Projects) Ltd
24A High Street
Ribben Village
Sedgedown SD7 4NO   3 September 20X5

Dear Sir (Madam)

Settlement of an amount of £822.50 in respect of goods supplied to you during June is still outstanding. If you have any queries regarding this amount, then please contact us as soon as possible to resolve any problems.

I must inform you that we are unable to accept further orders from you until your account is settled. If payment is not forthcoming, then we will find it necessary to take further action on this matter.

Yours faithfully

Jill Regan
Managing Director

Letter to Babbage & Lovelace

**Apparat Limited
7A Meadsway
Sedgedown
SD1 2ND**

Babbage & Lovelace
2 Telford Way
Ocset
SD3 9DA   3 September 20X5

Dear Sirs

I write to remind you that £440.25 of your balance with us now exceeds the 30-day credit period allowed. The remaining £58.75 of your balance becomes due for payment on 6 September.

I look forward to receiving full settlement of your balance by 6 September.

Yours faithfully

Jill Regan
Managing Director

Note. Babbage & Lovelace appears to be a partnership rather than a limited company and it is therefore more appropriate to address the letter to the partners together.

Answers to trial run devolved assessments

ANSWERS TO TRIAL RUN
DEVOLVED ASSESSMENT 1

ANSWERS

PART 1 - BARKERS

Task 1: **Cheques received listing**

Task 2: **Credit card summary voucher**

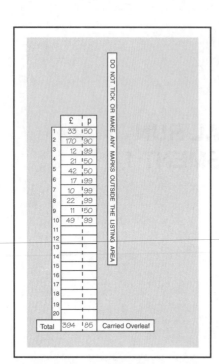

CHEQUE LISTING		BARKERS LIMITED	
DATE	1 5	20 X5	
NAME		ACCOUNT	AMOUNT
Poochy Pet Shop		P009	1,255.48
It's a Dog's Life		I008	79.94
Pet Superstore		P013	204.40
Pet Parlour		P027	827.00
TOTAL			2366.82

HAVE YOU IMPRINTED THE SUMMARY
WITH YOUR RETAILER'S CARD?

BANK Processing (White) copy of
Summary with your Vouchers in
correct order:
1. SUMMARY
2. SALES VOUCHERS
3. REFUND VOUCHERS

	ITEMS	AMOUNT	
SALES VOUCHERS (LISTED OVERLEAF)	10	394	85
LESS REFUND VOUCHERS			
DATE 1/5/X5	TOTAL	394	85

SUMMARY - RETAILER'S COPY

Crufts Bank **BANKING**
FASTPASS **SUMMARY**

- - - - - - - - - -
RETAILER'S SIGNATURE

COMPLETE THIS SUMMARY FOR EVERY DEPOSIT OF SALES VOUCHERS AND ENTER THE
TOTAL ON YOUR NORMAL CURRENT ACCOUNT PAYING-IN SLIP

Task 3: Paying-in slip

Date	1 May 20X5	
A/c	30595713	

Date 1 May 20X5

Cashier's stamp and initials

Notes	£50		
	£20		
	£10		
	£5		
Coins	£1		
	50p		
	20p		
	Silver		
	Bronze		
Cash £		815	79
Cheques		2897	33
£		3713	12

Fee

No of Cheques
11

bank giro credit

Paid in by/Customer's Reference

6 | 83048231 | 92057419 |

National Wetminster Bank

FIRST AVENUE BRANCH

NEWTONS LIMITED

Please do not write or mark below this line

Notes	£50		
	£20		
	£10		
	£5		
Coins	£1		
	50p		
	20p		
	Silver		
	Bronze		
Cash £		815	79
Cheques		2897	33
	£	3713	12

101131   ⑈101131⑈ 20⑈2748⑈ 30595713⑈

Details of Cheques, etc.			Sub-Total brought forward	135	66		17	50
							22	99
Mrs I Whippet	17	50	Poochy Pet Shop	1255	48		13	99
Mr J Corgi	22	99	It's A Dogs Life	79	94		13	50
Miss L Scott	13	99	Pet Superstore	204	40		17	68
Mr & Mrs N Hound	13	50	Pet Parlour	827	00		50	00
Miss A Mutt	17	68	Fastpass Credit Card Co	394	85		1255	48
Mr B Pup	50	00					79	94
							204	40
							827	00
							394	85
Carried Forward **£**	135	66	**Total** Carried over **£**	2897	33			
							2897	33

In view of the risk of loss in course of clearing, customers are advised to keep an independent record of the drawers of cheques

Please do not write or mark below this line

BPP PUBLISHING

Task 4:

			Discounts given		Total		VAT		Debtors		Cash Sales		Other receipts	
1		Brought forward			5672	50								
2	WK 1	Cash sales			130	70	19	47			111	23		
3		Cheque sales			54	48	8	11			46	37		
4		Credit card sales			238	89	35	58			203	31		
5														
6	WK 2	Cash sales			98	50	14	67			83	83		
7		Cheque sales			31	18	4	64			26	54		
8		Credit card sales			71	48	10	65			60	83		
9														
10	WK 3	Cash sales			572	60	85	28			487	32		
11		Cheque sales			50	00	7	45			42	55		
12		Credit card sales			22	99	3	42			19	57		
13														
14	WK 4	Cash sales			13	99	2	08			11	91		
15		Credit card sales			61	49	9	16			52	33		
16		Debtors	21	06	2366	82			2366	82				
17														
18		Deposit account interest			79	87							79	87
19														
20														
21														
22														
			21	06	9465	49	200	51	2366	82	1145	79	79	87

Task 5

Debtors control account

Date	Details	Amount £	Date	Details	Amount £
1 April 20X5	Balance b/f	Nil	30 April 20X5	Sales returns day book	235 57
30 April 20X5	Sales day book	2,623 45	30 April 20X5	Cash book	2,366 82
			30 April 20X5	Discounts allowed	21 06
			30 April 20X5	Balance c/f	Nil
		2,623 45			2,623 45
1 May 20X5	Balance b/f	Nil			

Sales

Date	Details	Amount £	Date	Details	Amount £
30 April 20X5	Sales returns day book	235.57	1 April 20X5	Balance b/f	6,826.30
			30 April 20X5	Sales day book	2,623.45
30 April 20X5	Balance c/f	10,359.97	30 April 20X5	Cash book	1,145.79
		10,595.54			10,595.54
			1 May 20X5	Balance b/f	10,359.97

Bank interest received

Date	Details	Amount £	Date	Details	Amount £
			1 April 20X5	Balance b/f	284.50
30 April 20X5	Balance c/f	364.37	30 April 20X5	Cash book	79.87
		364.37			364.37
			1 May 20X5		364.37

VAT

Date	Details	Amount £	Date	Details	Amount £
30 April 20X5	Purchase day book	181 43	1 April 20X5	Balance b/f	586 48
			30 April 20X5	Sales day book	352 51
			30 April 20X5	Cash book	200 51
30 April 20X5	Balance c/f	958 07			
		1,139 50			1,139 50
			1 May 20X5	Balance b/f	898 81

Discounts allowed

Date	Details	Amount £	Date	Details	Amount £
1 April 20X5	Balance b/f	67 42	30 April 20X5	Balance c/f	88 48
30 April 20X5	Debtors control a/c	21 06			
		88 48			88 48
1 May 20X5	Balance b/f	88 48			

BPP PUBLISHING

Task 6: Bank reconciliation at 30 April 20X5

	£	£
Balance per bank statement		4,248.15
Add outstanding lodgements (note)		3,713.12
Less cheques not yet presented *paid out*		
101096	101.01	
101101	336.10	
101102	813.72	
101103	75.35	
101104	16.22	
101105	352.60	
101106	157.02	
		(1,852.02)
		6,109.25

2 ends

Note. This amount comprises all receipts in April except interest.

Bal per BS

ASSESSMENT CRITERIA

Task 1

The cheque listing must be accurately prepared. No more than one error allowed.

Task 2

Credit card sales must be correctly recorded on the summary voucher. No more than one error allowed.

Task 3

As Tasks 1 and 2.

Task 4

Cash receipts must be correctly entered and totalled. No more than two calculation errors allowed.

Task 5

Totals posted to the nominal ledger accounts. Only one error allowed.

Task 6

Reconciliation correctly prepared. Two minor errors allowed.

PART 2 - BEST BOOKS

TASK 1

Best-Books Ltd	No _____ *R107* _____ Best-Books Ltd _____ *12/05* 20 *X7*
No _____ *R107* _____	Received with _____ *Fourteen* _____ pounds
_____ *12/05* 20 *X7* _____	thanks the sum of _____ *51* _____ pence
	~~cheque~~/cash
£ _____ *14.51p* _____	£ _____ *14.51* _____ Signature _____ *A Murray*

Best-Books Ltd	No _____ *R108* _____ Best-Books Ltd _____ *12/05* 20 *X7*
No _____ *R108* _____	Received with _____ *Twenty seven* _____ pounds
_____ *12/05* 20 *X7* _____	thanks the sum of _____ *99* _____ pence
	cheque/~~cash~~
£ _____ *27.99p* _____	£ _____ *27.99* _____ Signature _____ *A Murray*

Best-Books Ltd	No _____ *R109* _____ Best-Books Ltd _____ *12/05* 20 *X7*
No _____ *R109* _____	Received with _____ *Fifty eight* _____ pounds
_____ *12/05* 20 *X7* _____	thanks the sum of _____ *99* _____ pence
	cheque/~~cash~~
£ _____ *58.99p* _____	£ _____ *58.99* _____ Signature _____ *A Murray*

Best-Books Ltd

No _____R110_____

_____12/05_____ 20 __X7__

£ _____14.40p_____

No _____R110_____ Best-Books Ltd _____12/05_____ 20 __X7__

Received with
thanks the
sum of

_____Fourteen_____ pounds

_____40_____ pence

~~cheque~~/cash

£ __14.40__ Signature _____A Murray_____

Best-Books Ltd

No _____R111_____

_____12/05_____ 20 __X7__

£ _____17.46p_____

No _____R111_____ Best-Books Ltd _____12/05_____ 20 __X7__

Received with
thanks the
sum of

_____Seventeen_____ pounds

_____46_____ pence

cheque/~~cash~~

£ __17.46__ Signature _____A Murray_____

Best-Books Ltd

No _____R112_____

_____12/05_____ 20 __X7__

£ _____11.46p_____

No _____R112_____ Best-Books Ltd _____12/05_____ 20 __X7__

Received with
thanks the
sum of

_____Eleven_____ pounds

_____46_____ pence

~~cheque~~/cash

£ __11.46__ Signature _____A Murray_____

TASK 2

PRESTON SHOP	DATE: 12/05/X7	
	£	£
Float at start of day		30.00
Receipts for day		
Cash	79.11	
Cheque	214.83	
Credit card	202.47	
Total		496.41
Less: Float required		(30.00)
Credit card transactions		(202.47)
Amount to be banked		293.94

TASK 3

	Notes			Coins						
	£20	£10	£5	£1	50p	20p	10p	5p	2p	1p
Opening float		2	1	2	2	3	2	4	40	20
+ Total received in day	1	4	3	16	2	2	0	0	0	1
– Total paid in change	0	0	1	6	2	3	2	4	10	10
– Float required		2	1	4	1	1	0	0	10	10
Total to be banked										
Number	1	4	2	8	1	1	0	0	20	1
Value £	20.00	40.00	10.00	8.00	0.50	0.20	0	0	0.40	0.01

BPP PUBLISHING

TASK 4

Date	12/05/X7	

bank giro credit 🏦
Paid in by/Customer's Reference

Date 12/05/X7

£50 notes		-
£20 notes	20	00
£10 notes	40	00
£5 notes	10	00
£1	8	00
50p	0	50
20p	0	20
10p		-
5p		-
Bronze	0	41
Total		
Cash	79	11
Cheques (see over)	214	83
£	293	94

Code No: 30-60-58
Bank: Lancs Bank PLC
Branch: Preston

Credit: BEST BOOKS LTD
Account No: 60711348

Number
of
Cheques

Paid in by A Murray

£50 notes		-
£20 notes	20	00
£10 notes	40	00
£5 notes	10	00
£1	8	00
50p	0	50
20p	0	20
10p		-
5p		-
Bronze	0	41
Total		
Cash	79	11
Cheques (see over)	214	83
£	293	94

Cheque analysis		Counterfoil	
Customer No	£	Customer No	£
3	10.50	3	10.50
6	13.54	6	13.54
7	27.99	7	27.99
8	58.99	8	58.99
12	21.90	12	21.90
16	17.46	16	17.46
20	64.45	20	64.45
	214.83		214.83

TASK 5

Cheques and remittance advices received	Action
P Davies Ltd	The words and figures on the cheque are different. The figures should read £684.50. Refer to P Davies Ltd.
J Davidson Ltd	Cheque is dated '20X6' not '20X7' and £6.90 on remittance advice has not been ticked off as included in payment. Refer to J Davidson Ltd.
A Tatlock plc	No corrective action needed.
M Pagan Ltd	No corrective action needed.

TASK 6

Sales ledger

A TATLOCK PLC

		£			£
1 April	Bal b/d	197.38	16 April	Bank	97.38
17 April	Sales	210.51	24 April	Bank	310.51
27 April	Sales	192.40	30 April	Bal c/d	192.40
		600.29			600.29
1 May	Bal b/d	192.40			

P DAVIES PLC

		£			£
1 April	Bal b/d	-	17 April	Bank	194.30
3 April	Sales	294.30	21 April	Bank	151.37
14 April	Sales	151.37			
27 April	Sales	684.50	30 April	Bal c/d	784.50
		1,130.17			1,130.17
1 May	Bal b/d	784.50			

TASK 7

Two column cash book

Date	Details	Cash	Bank	Date	Details	Cash	Bank
		£	£			£	£
1/4/X7	Bal b/d	21.90		1/4/X7	Bal b/d		101.45
3/4/X7	Debtors		1,016.94	2/4/X7	Sundry payments	11.50	2,165.83
7/4/X7	Sales	394.60					
8/4/X7	Contra		200.00	8/4/X7	Contra	200.00	
13/4/X7	Debtors		440.50	19/4/X7	Contra	300.00	
18/4/X7	Sales	264.66					
19/4/X7	Contra		300.00	28/4/X7	Contra	100.00	
22/4/X7	Debtors		760.00				
28/4/X7	Contra		100.00	30/4/X7	Bal c/d	69.66	550.16
		681.16	2,817.44			681.16	2,817.44
1/5/X7	Bal b/d	69.66	550.16				

ASSESSMENT CRITERIA

Task 1

The six receipts should be filled in accurately and neatly. No more than one error may be allowed.

Task 2

The takings schedule must be accurate with no mistakes.

Task 3

The cash reconciliation sheet must be filled in accurately and the correct totals included.

Task 4

The bank paying in slip must be accurate. No more than one error permitted.

Task 5

The two errors on P Davies Ltd and J Davidson Ltd must be spotted, and identified as errors.

Task 6

The ledger must be completed accurately and balances carried down to the next period of account.

Task 7

The two column cash book must be filled in neatly and accurately. Not more than one error permitted.

Overall assessment

You may be allowed to make further minor errors, provided you do not suggest a fundamental lack of understanding.

You will not be penalised more than once for the same error. If you transfer an incorrect figure to another part of the exercise, this is not counted as a further error.

ANSWERS TO TRIAL RUN
DEVOLVED ASSESSMENT 2

**DO NOT TURN THIS PAGE UNTIL YOU HAVE
COMPLETED THE TRIAL RUN DEVOLVED ASSESSMENT**

ANSWERS

PART 1 - GROW EASY

TASK 1

No	R202		No	R202	Grow-Easy	24/04 20 X7

No   R202

24/04   20   X7

From   J Alexander

£ 341.72

No   R202   Grow-Easy   24/04   20   X7

Received from   J Alexander

the sum of   three hundered and forty one   pounds

seventy two   pence

~~cheque~~/~~cash~~

£ 341.72   Signature   *S Dutton*

No   R203

24/04   20   X7

From   C Hall

£ 17.46

No   R203   Grow-Easy   24/04   20   X7

Received from   C Hall

the sum of   seventeen   pounds

forty six   pence

~~cheque~~/cash

£ 17.46   Signature   *S Dutton*

No   R204

24/04   20   X7

From   S Hill

£ 23.40

No   R204   Grow-Easy   24/04   20   X7

Received from   S Hill

the sum of   twenty three   pounds

forty   pence

~~cheque~~/cash

£ 23.40   Signature   *S Dutton*

:

No ___R205___	No ___R205___ Grow-Easy ___24/04___ 20 _X7_
___24/04___ 20 _X7_	Received from ___J Dawson___
From ___J Dawson___	the sum of ___fourteen___ pounds
	___thirty six___ pence
	cheque/~~cash~~
£ ___14.36___	£ 14.36 Signature ___S Dutton___

No ___R206___	No ___R206___ Grow-Easy ___24/04___ 20 _X7_
___24/04___ 20 _X7_	Received from ___M Wright___
From ___M Wright___	the sum of ___one hundred and one___ pounds
	___twenty six___ pence
	cheque/~~cash~~
£ ___101.26___	£ 101.26 Signature ___S Dutton___

No ___R207___	No ___R207___ Grow-Easy ___24/04___ 20 _X7_
___24/04___ 20 _X7_	Received from ___I Clinton___
From ___I Clinton___	the sum of ___ninety four___ pounds
	___seventy eight___ pence
	cheque/~~cash~~
£ ___94.78___	£ 94.78 Signature ___S Dutton___

TASK 2

Date	Customer	Amount £	Method Cash/cheque	Invoice No
24.4.X7	J Alexander	341.72	cheque	B741
24.4.X7	C Hall	17.46	cash	B726
24.4.X7	S Hill	23.40	cash	B749
24.4.X7	J Dawson	14.36	cheque	B801
24.4.X7	M Wright	101.26	cheque	B794
24.4.X7	I Clinton	94.78	cheque	B797
24.4.X7	P Phillips	79.46	cheque	B646
24.4.X7	S Lee	296.30	cheque	B793
24.4.X7	S Churchward	27.37	cheque	B699
24.4.X7	C Drury	74.90	cheque	B785
		£1,071.01		

		£
Total:	cash	40.86
	cheque	1,030.15
		1,071.01

TASK 3

	Notes			Coins						
	£20	*£10*	*£5*	*£1*	*50p*	*20p*	*10p*	*5p*	*2p*	*1p*
Cash till										
1	2	4	2	10	6	40	16	21	84	70
2	3	6	2	18	4	21	49	40	71	60
3	1	2	1	4	2	10	36	30	44	39
4	1	5	3	9	1	11	15	8	27	68
Total	7	17	8	41	13	82	116	99	226	237
Less: Float required	(--)	(4)	(4)	(20)	(8)	(--)	(80)	(80)	(160)	(80)
To be banked										
Number	7	13	4	21	5	82	36	19	66	157
Value £	£140.00	£130.00	£20.00	£21.00	£2.50	£16.40	£3.60	£0.95	£1.32	£1.57

TASK 4

Date __24/04/X7__			**bank giro credit**			
			Paid in by/Customer's Reference			
			Date __24/04/X7__			
£50 notes	-			£50 notes	-	
£20 notes	140	00	Code No: 40-70-68	£20 notes	140	00
£10 notes	130	00	Bank: Cumbria Bank PLC	£10 notes	130	00
£5 notes	20	00	Branch: Kendal	£5 notes	20	00
£1	21	00		£1	21	00
50p	2	50	Credit: **GROW-EASY LTD**	50p	2	50
20p	16	40	Account No: 40711396	20p	16	40
10p	3	60		10p	3	60
5p	0	95	Number of Cheques	5p	0	95
Bronze	2	89	8	Bronze	2	89
Total				Total		
Cash	337	34		Cash	337	34
Cheques (see over)	1030	15		Cheques (see over)	1030	15
£	1367	49	Paid in by _S Dutton_	£	1367	49

Cheque analysis			Counterfoil	
Name	Invoice No	£	Name	£
J Alexander	B741	341.72	J Alexander	341.72
J Dawson	B801	14.36	J Dawson	14.36
M Wright	B794	101.26	M Wright	101.26
I Clinton	B797	94.78	I Clinton	94.78
P Phillips	B646	79.46	P Phillips	79.46
S Lee	B793	296.30	S Lee	296.30
S Churchward	B699	27.37	S Churchward	27.37
C Drury	B785	74.90	C Drury	74.90
		1030.15		1030.15

TASK 5

Standing orders	Action
Northern Gas Board	The bank statement has a standing order charge which differs from the standing order details. I would check with the accountant and the bank, if necessary, to resolve the discrepancy. (£1,260.00 ÷ 12 = £105)

TASK 6

BANK RECONCILIATION STATEMENT AS AT 3.3.X7

	£	£
Balance as per cash book		3,894.65
Less standing orders:		
Electricity Board	(79.00)	
Gas Board	(105.00)	
BT	(200.00)	
		(384.00)
Add unpresented cheques at 31.3.X7		894.72
Less: uncredited income		(596.40)
Add: standing order discrepancy to be resolved		10.00
Balance as per bank statement		3,818.97

ASSESSMENT CRITERIA

Task 1

The six receipts should be filled in accurately and neatly. No more than one error may be allowed.

Task 2

The payments received analysis form must be filled in accurately and neatly and the totals included. No more than one error may be allowed.

Task 3

The cash reconciliation sheet must be filled in accurately and the correct totals included.

Task 4

The bank paying in slip must be accurate. No more than one error permitted.

Task 5

The Gas Board standing order must be identified as an error.

Task 6

Only a correct reconciliation is enough to demonstrate competence.

Overall assessment

Students may be allowed to make further minor errors, provided they do not suggest a fundamental lack of understanding.

Students must not be penalised more than once for the same error. If a student transfers an incorrect figure to another part of the exercise, this is not counted as a further error.

BPP
PUBLISHING

PART 2 - WORKBASE OPFFICE SUPPLIES

TASK 1

WORKBASE OFFICE SUPPLIES LTD

MEMORANDUM

To: Mr Denton
From: A Technician
Re: *VAT and discounts*

You have asked me to explain how VAT is calculated when discounts are offered to customers.

Value added tax is charged on the lowest amount which a customer can pay. Thus, if a trade or bulk discount is offered, as it is in the case of Workbase, then this is deducted before VAT is calculated.

Any cash or settlement discount (2% for Workbase) is also deducted to arrive at the lowest amount payable, and 17.5% VAT is calculated on this latter amount.

For example, a customer who is entitled to a trade discount of 20% buys goods priced at £125. He is invoiced as follows.

	£
Goods at list price	125.00
Discount 20%	25.00
	100.00
VAT (17.5% × £98.00)	17.15
	117.15

The customer may either pay £117.15 or, if paying within 14 days, £98 plus £17.15 VAT = £115.15.

I hope this explains the situation fully. We need to ensure that the accounts department understands these principles.

TASK 2

Invoice details which have been corrected are underlined.

WORKBASE OFFICE SUPPLIES LTD   Invoice No. *894*

    63 Conduit Street
Liverpool L1 6NN

Telephone: 0151-432 2222
Fax: 0151-432 2210

VAT Reg No. 924 4614 29

Account No.   *C011*

Date/Tax point *22 August 20X5*

Coals of Newcastle Ltd
25A Hive Street
Newcastle-upon-Tyne
NE4 6PR

Product code	Description	Quantity	Unit price £ p	Total amount £ p
F58110	Ambico 6-shelf unit	4	126.00	504.00
F10577	Ambience 9-drawer cabinet	2	484.50	969.00
A89811	Priory system tray sets (grey)	6	14.27	85.62
			Goods total: less 10% discount:	1558.62 155.86

Comments:	NET TOTAL	1402.76
2% settlement discount for payment within 14 days of invoice date	VAT @ 17.5%	240.57
	TOTAL	1643.33

Registered office: 63 Conduit Street, Liverpool L1 6NN   Registered No: 822 4742

Note. VAT = £1,402.76 x 98% x 17.5% = £240.57

WORKBASE OFFICE SUPPLIES LTD

63 Conduit Street
Liverpool L1 6NN

Telephone: 0151-432 2222
Fax: 0151-432 2210

VAT Reg No. 924 4614 29

Invoice No. 895

Account No.   B020

Date/Tax point 22 August 20X5

Bowser & Bowser
22 Canard Lane
Duckley
SR1 1RF

Product code	Description	Quantity	Unit price £ p	Total amount £ p
G12352	Packs black med. Ultrapoint	50	6.08	304.00
G14000	Packs HB Office Star pencils	24	2.58	61.92
A22588	600F 4-hole fixed punch	20	20.47	409.40
G14384	Two colour Hi-Lite Jumbo marker	120	1.71	205.20
G14393	Fine red Hi-Lite Jumbo marker	30	0.94	28.20
			Goods total: less 25% discount:	1008.72 252.18

Comments:	NET TOTAL	756.54
2% settlement discount for payment within 14 days of invoice date	VAT @ 17.5%	129.74
	TOTAL	886.28

Registered office: 63 Conduit Street, Liverpool L1 6NN   Registered No: 822 4742

Note.   VAT = £756.54 x 98% x 17.5% = £129.74

WORKBASE OFFICE SUPPLIES LTD

63 Conduit Street
Liverpool L1 6NN

Telephone: 0151-432 2222
Fax: 0151-432 2210

VAT Reg No. 924 4614 29

Invoice No. *896*

Account No.   U001

Date/Tax point 22 August 20X5

Underwood Dairies
Milk Street
Kingston
SR7 4NR

Product code	Description	Quantity	Unit price £ p	Total amount £ p
F71610	Chequers 474E chair (Oatmeal)	1	136.00	136.00
F74700	Exeter 420L chair (Oatmeal)	2	296.00	592.00
F10420	Ambience multidrawer cabinets (Grey)	4	186.20	744.80
F55550	600 workstation base unit	1	85.15	85.15
			Goods total: less 20% discount:	1557.95 311.59

Comments:

2% settlement discount for
payment within 14 days of invoice date

NET TOTAL	1246.36
VAT @ 17.5%	213.75
TOTAL	1460.11

Registered office: 63 Conduit Street, Liverpool L1 6NN   Registered No: 822 4742

Note.   VAT = £1246.36 x 98% x 17.5% = £213.75

BPP
PUBLISHING

WORKBASE OFFICE SUPPLIES LTD

**63 Conduit Street
Liverpool L1 6NN**

Credit Note No. C451

Telephone: 0151-432 2222
Fax: 0151-432 2210

VAT Reg No. 924 4614 29

Account No.   U001

Date/Tax point   22 August 20X5

Underwood Dairies
Milk Street
Kingston
SR7 4NR

Product code	Description	Quantity	Unit price £ p	Total amount £ p
A87821	Tower 300 filing trays	10	4.92	49.20
A87822	Tower 400 filing trays	15	6.13	91.95
			Goods total:	141.15
			Less 20% discount:	28.23
Comments:			NET TOTAL	112.92
	Returned goods (original invoice no. 872)		VAT @ 17.5%	19.36
			TOTAL	132.28

Registered office: 63 Conduit Street, Liverpool L1 6NN   Registered No: 822 4742

Note.   VAT = £112.92 x 98% x 17.5% = £19.36

TASK 3

WORKBASE OFFICE SUPPLIES LTD

SALES DAY BOOK

Date	Invoice/CN No.	Customer No.	Total	A	F	G	Sundry Sales	VAT
22.8.X5	894	C011	1643.33	77.06	1325.70			240.57
22.8.X5	895	B020	886.28	307.05		449.49		129.74
22.8.X5	896	U001	1460.11		1246.36			213.75
22.8.X5	C451	U001	(132.28)	(112.92)				(19.36)
	TOTAL		3857.44	271.19	2572.06	449.49		564.70

WORKBASE OFFICE SUPPLIES LTD

no 801

Ledger Postings

Date of transactions: 22 August 20X5

Account name	Account code	NOMINAL LEDGER DR £ p	NOMINAL LEDGER CR £ p	MEMORANDUM ACCOUNTS DR £ p	MEMORANDUM ACCOUNTS CR £ p
Sales ledger control	2000	3857.44			
894 - Coals of Newcastle	C011			1643.33	
855 - Bowser & Bowser	B020			886.28	
896 - Underwood Dairies	U001			1460.11	
C451 - Underwood Daries	U001				132.28
Sales A	5710		271.19		
Sales F	5720		2572.06		
Sales G	5730		449.49		
VAT control	3500	19.36	584.06		
Totals		3876.80	3876.80	3989.72	132.28

Authorised by _____ date _____

Posted by _____ date _____

Note. There is no separate sales returns day book. £3,857.44 is the figure net of returns which is posted from the sales day book.

TASK 4

WORKBASE OFFICE SUPPLIES LTD

no 802

Ledger Postings

Date of transactions: 22 August 20X5

Account name	Account code	NOMINAL LEDGER		MEMORANDUM ACCOUNTS	
		DR £ p	CR £ p	DR £ p	CR £ p
Sales ledger control	2000		321.70		
Meadwaite Ltd	M070				321.70
Bad debts expense	6350	321.70			
Sales ledger control	2000		94.00		
Purchase ledger control	3000	94.00			
Spooner Ltd	801S			94.00	
Spooner Ltd	S700				94.00
Totals		415.70	415.70	94.00	415.70

Authorised by _____ date _____

Posted by _____ date _____

BPP
PUBLISHING

ASSESSMENT CRITERIA

Task 1

Full and correct explanation of VAT treatment. Only one calculation error allowed in examples.

Task 2

Errors in invoices should be correctly identified. Only two errors or omissions allowed. Credit note correctly completed with only one error allowed.

Task 3

Items correctly recorded in sales day book. Only one error allowed. Postings to the general ledger correct and accurate. Only two errors allowed.

Task 4

Write off and contra-entry correctly posted.

ANSWERS TO TRIAL RUN
DEVOLVED ASSESSMENT 3

**DO NOT TURN THIS PAGE UNTIL YOU HAVE
COMPLETED THE TRIAL RUN DEVOLVED ASSESSMENT**

ANSWERS

PART 1: PAPER PRODUCTS

TASK 1

Sales invoice check - invoice number	Action
2507	Invoice correct - no action required.
2508	Labels have been incorrectly priced at £19.50 rather than £17.50. Re-issue a correct sales invoice.
2509	The VAT has been calculated on the figures before discount rather than the figure after discount. Re-issue a correct sales invoice.

TASK 2

PAPER PRODUCTS LTD

139 Garstang Road, Preston PR1 8HG
Tel: 01772 604007   Fax: 01772 604931

SALES INVOICE   Invoice No.   2510

VAT No.: 220 5564 12   Date/Tax point: 30.5.X7

Item Description	Code	Quantity	Unit price	Total
			£ p	£ p
Disc boxes (10)	604	2	19.50	39.00
Computer paper (2000)	617	5	34.70	173.50
Highlighters (pink)	696	10	10.20	102.00
Memo pads (A4)	703	4	17.40	69.60

Total Trade discount (%) -5%	384.10 (19.21)
Net VAT @ 17.5%	364.89 63.86
Amount due	428.75

To: Consumer Products Ltd
      105 Coventry Road
      Walsall
      B12 0EP

PAPER PRODUCTS LTD

139 Garstang Road, Preston PR1 8HG
Tel: 01772 604007   Fax: 01772 604931

SALES INVOICE			Invoice No.	2511
VAT No.: 220 5564 12			Date/Tax point:	30.5.X7

Item Description	Code	Quantity	Unit price	Total
			£ p	£ p
Labels (5000)	629	8	17.50	140.00
Ring binders (black)	652	3	26.20	78.60
Paperclips (small)	676	14	1.80	25.20
Pens (green)	681	5	8.90	44.50

Total	288.30
Trade discount (%) -7.5%	(21.62)
Net	266.68
VAT @ 17.5%	46.67
Amount due	313.35

To: Stationery Stores Ltd
     16 Greenbank Road
     Ipswich
     IP32 4QD

PAPER PRODUCTS LTD

139 Garstang Road, Preston PR1 8HG
Tel: 01772 604007   Fax: 01772 604931

SALES INVOICE

VAT No.: 220 5564 12

Invoice No.   2512

Date/Tax point: 30.5.X7

Item Description	Code	Quantity	Unit price £ p	Total £ p
Computer paper (1006)	612	4	18.45	73.80
Labels (5000)	629	6	17.50	105.00
Ring binders (other)	654	2	28.10	56.20
Highlighters (yellow)	694	9	10.50	94.50

Total	329.50
Trade discount (%) -10%	(32.95)
Net	296.55
VAT @ 17.5%	51.90
Amount due	348.45

To: Clinton and Wright Distribution Ltd
      201 Eastgate Road
      Bristol
      BS1 2HD

TASK 3

PAPER PRODUCTS LTD

139 Garstang Road, Preston PR1 8HG
Tel: 01772 604007   Fax: 01772 604931

CREDIT NOTE

CREDIT NOTE TO:

Alexander Ltd
201 Blackburn Road
Bolton
BL1 2HE

Vat reg: 220 5564 12
Date/tax point: 30.5.X7
Credit note no: 117

ITEM DESCRIPTION	CODE	QUANTITY	UNIT PRICE	TOTAL
Disc box (10)	604	1	19.50	19.50
Highlighters (yellow)	694	1	10.50	10.50
Total				30.00
Trade discount (10%)				(3.00)
Net				27.00
VAT at 17.5%				4.73
Total credit				31.73

PAPER PRODUCTS LTD

139 Garstang Road, Preston PR1 8HG
Tel: 01772 604007   Fax: 01772 604931

CREDIT NOTE

CREDIT NOTE TO:

Stationery Stores Ltd
16 Greenbank Road
Ipswich
IP32 4QP

Vat reg: 220 5564 12
Date/tax point: 30.5.X7
Credit note no: 118

ITEM DESCRIPTION	CODE	QUANTITY	UNIT PRICE	TOTAL
Pens (green)	681	2	8.90	17.80
Total				17.80
Trade discount (7.5%)				(1.34)
Net				16.46
VAT at 17.5%				2.88
Total credit				19.34

TASK 4

PAPER PRODUCTS LIMITED
SALES DAY BOOK

Date	Invoice	Customer	Total £	VAT £	Boxes/binders/ files £	Paperclips/ labels £	Envelopes/ paper/pads £	Maker pens/ highlighters £
29.5.X7 b/d		Alexander	224.42	33.42	106.00	25.00	40.00	20.00
		Consumer Products	227.54	33.89	25.90	131.15	19.20	17.40
		Halton Group	72.38	10.78	-	-	12.00	49.60
		Ronald Davies	147.87	22.02	17.60	-	-	108.25
		Stationery Stores	100.58	14.98	36.20	49.40	-	-
		Clinton & Wright	94.94	14.14	29.00	17.00	-	34.80
30.5.X7	2507	Alexander	251.26	37.42	117.90	13.86	82.08	-
	2508	Consumer Products	472.70	70.40	-	47.25	209.25	145.80
	2509	Halton Group	644.86	96.04	336.06	-	212.76	-
	2510	Ronald Davies	428.75	63.86	37.05	164.82	66.12	96.90
	2511	Stationery Stores	313.35	46.67	72.71	152.81	-	41.16
	2512	Clinton & Wright	348.45	51.90	50.58	94.50	66.42	85.05

SALES RETURNS DAY BOOK

Date	Credit note	Customer	Total £	VAT £	Boxes/binders/ files £	Paperclips/ labels £	Envelopes/ paper/pads £	Maker pens/ highlighters £
29.5.X7 b/d			-	-	-	-	-	-
30.5.X7	117	Alexander	31.73	4.73	17.55	-	-	9.45
30.5.X7	118	Stationery Stores	19.34	2.88	-	-	-	16.46

BPP PUBLISHING

TASK 5

SALES LEDGER

ACCOUNT: ALEXANDER LTD					
Date	*Details*	*£*	*Date*	*Details*	*£*
29.5.X7	b/d	224.43	30.5.X7	Credit note 117	31.73
30.5.X7	Invoice 2507	251.26			

ACCOUNT: HALTON GROUP LTD					
Date	*Details*	*£*	*Date*	*Details*	*£*
29.5.X7	b/d	72.38			
30.5.X7	Invoice 2508	472.70			

ACCOUNT: RONALD DAVIES DISTRIBUTION					
Date	*Details*	*£*	*Date*	*Details*	*£*
29.5.X7	b/d	147.87			
30.5.X7	Invoice 2509	644.86			

ACCOUNT: CONSUMER PRODUCTS LTD					
Date	*Details*	*£*	*Date*	*Details*	*£*
29.5.X7	b/d	227.54			
30.5.X7	Invoice 2510	428.75			

ACCOUNT: STATIONERY STORES LTD					
Date	*Details*	*£*	*Date*	*Details*	*£*
29.5.X7	b/d	100.58	30.5.X7	Credit note 118	19.34
30.5.X7	Invoice 2511	313.35			

ACCOUNT: CLINTON AND WRIGHT LTD					
Date	*Details*	*£*	*Date*	*Details*	*£*
29.5.X7	b/d	94.94			
30.5.X7	Invoice 2512	348.45			

TASK 6

NOMINAL (GENERAL) LEDGER

ACCOUNT: SALES LEDGER CONTROL					
Date	*Details*	£	*Date*	*Details*	£
29.5.X7	b/d	867.73	30.5.X7	Sales returns day book	51.07
30.5.X7	Sales day book	2,459.37			

ACCOUNT: VAT CONTROL					
Date	*Details*	£	*Date*	*Details*	£
30.5.X7	Sales returns day book	7.61	29.5.X7	b/d	129.24
			30.5.X7	Sales day book	366.29

ACCOUNT: SALES - BOXES, BINDERS, FILES					
Date	*Details*	£	*Date*	*Details*	£
30.5.X7	Sales returns day book	17.55	29.5.X7	b/d	214.70
			30.5.X7	Sales day book	614.30

ACCOUNT: SALES - PAPERCLIPS, LABELS					
Date	*Details*	£	*Date*	*Details*	£
			29.5.X7	b/d	222.55
			30.5.X7	Sales day book	473.24

ACCOUNT: SALES – ENVELOPES, PAPER, PADS					
Date	*Details*	£	*Date*	*Details*	£
			29.5.X7	b/d	71.20
			30.5.X7	Sales day book	636.63

ACCOUNT: SALES – PENS, MARKERS, HIGHLIGHERS					
Date	*Details*	£	*Date*	*Details*	£
30.5.X7	Sales returns day book	25.91	29.5.X7	b/d	230.05
			30.5.X7	Sales day book	368.91

ASSESSMENT CRITERIA

Task 1

The two incorrect invoices should be identified and the necessary corrective action noted.

Task 2

Invoices should be prepared accurately. No more than one arithmetical error allowed.

Task 3

Both credit notes must be accurately completed.

Task 4

The sales day book and sales returns day book must be accurately completed with no more than one error allowed.

Task 5

Details must be transferred accurately to the sales ledger accounts. All the relevant columns should be completed accurately and neatly.

Task 6

As Task 5 but the entries are into the general ledger accounts.

PART 2: CATERING CONTRACTS

TASK 1

INVOICE CALCULATION SHEET

Name	Details	Amount £	Less discount £	Net £	VAT £	Total £
Highland Hotels	2 at £195.99	391.98				
	36 at £14.50	522.00				
	16 at £34.00	544.00				
		1,457.98	(364.50)	1,093.48	191.36	1,284.84
Happy Eaters Group	8 at £34.00	272.00				
	1 at £297.60	297.60				
		569.60	(56.96)	512.64	89.71	602.35
Catering Consumables	6 at £7.49	44.94				
	2 at £9.99	19.98				
		64.92	(6.49)	58.43	10.23	68.66
Sneddons Ltd	11 at £9.99	109.89	(10.99)	98.90	17.31	116.21
Bensons Bakers	1 at £157.80	157.80				
	3 at £34.00	102.00				
	17 at £2.75	46.75				
		306.55	(30.66)	275.89	48.28	324.17
Easy-Fry Co	3 at £3.99	11.97				
	1 at £146.45	146.45				
	1 at £17.40	17.40				
		175.82	(26.37)	149.45	26.15	175.60
Peak Manufacturing	2 at £42.75	85.50				
	11 at £17.40	191.40				
	4 at £34.00	136.00				
	10 at £1.49	14.90				
		427.80	(85.56)	342.24	59.89	402.13
Beautiful Bakers	4 at £8.90	35.60				
	15 at £1.29	19.35				
		54.95	(5.50)	49.45	8.65	58.10
Totals		3,167.51	(587.03)	2,580.48	451.58	3,032.06

TASK 2

SALES DAY BOOK

Date	Name	Details	Invoice No	Goods £	VAT £	Total £
23 June	Highland Hotels	Cookers/utensils/cutlery	CC1027	1,093.48	191.36	1,284.84
23 June	Happy Eaters Group	Cutlery sets and hod	CC1028	512.64	89.71	602.35
24 June	Catering Consumables	Pans	CC1029	58.43	10.23	68.66
25 June	Sneddons Ltd	Pans	CC1030	98.90	17.31	116.21
25 June	Bensons Bakers	Hob/cutlery sets/baking trays	CC0131	275.89	48.28	324.17
25 June	Easy Fry Co	Pans/hob/kettle	CC1032	149.45	26.15	175.60
26 June	Peak Manufacturing	Pans/kettles/cutlery sets/glasses	CC0133	342.24	59.89	402.13
27 June	Beautiful Bakers	Table mats/glasses	CC0134	49.45	8.65	58.10
				2,580.48	451.58	3,032.06

TASK 3

SALES RETURNS DAY BOOK

Name	Details	Amount £	Less discount £	Net £	VAT £	Total £
Happy Eaters Group	Overcharge on glasses (72) - 60p per glass	43.20	(4.32)	38.88	6.80	45.68
Peak Manufacturing	Overcharge on invoice 2 cutlery sets	68.00	(13.60)	54.40	9.52	63.92
Totals		111.20	(17.92)	93.28	16.32	109.60

TASK 4

SALES LEDGER

HIGHLAND HOTELS

		£			£
June	Sales	1,284.84	c/d		1,284.84
b/d		1,284.84			

HAPPY EATERS GROUP

		£			£
June	Sales	602.35	June	Sales returns	45.68
			c/d		556.67
		602.35			602.35
b/d		556.67			

BPP
PUBLISHING

CATERING CONSUMABLES

		£			£
June	Sales	68.66	c/d		68.66
	b/d	68.66			

SNEDDONS LTD

		£			£
June	Sales	116.21	c/d		116.21
	b/d	116.21			

BENSONS BAKERS

		£			£
June	Sales	324.17	c/d		324.17
	b/d	324.17			

EASY FRY CO

		£			£
June	Sales	175.60	c/d		175.60
	b/d	175.60			

PEAK MANUFACTURING

		£			£
June	Sales	402.13	June	Sales returns	63.92
				c/d	338.21
		402.13			402.13
	b/d	338.21			

BEAUTIFUL BAKERS

		£			£
June	Sales	58.10	c/d		58.10
	b/d	58.10			

TASK 5

GENERAL LEDGER

SALES ACCOUNT

	£		£
Sales returns for June	93.28	Sales for June	2,580.48
c/d	2,487.20		
	2,580.48		2,580.48
		b/d	2,487.20

VAT ACCOUNT

	£		£
VAT on sales returns for June	16.32	VAT on sales for June	451.58
c/d	435.26		
	451.58		451.58
		b/d	435.26

TASK 6

GENERAL LEDGER

DEBTORS CONTROL ACCOUNT

	£		£
June sales	3,032.06	June sales returns	109.60
		c/d	2,922.46
	3,032.06		3,032.06
b/d	2,922.46		

BPP PUBLISHING

ASSESSMENT CRITERIA

Task 1

The invoice values should be calculated accurately and the discounts and VAT correctly applied. No more than two errors allowed.

Task 2

Figures produced in Task 1 should be correctly transferred to the sales day book.

Task 3

The details for the two sales returns day book items must be correctly calculated and transferred to the sales returns day book.

Task 4

The invoice values must be transferred correctly to the sales ledger. No more than one error allowed.

Tasks 5 & 6

As Task 4.

ORDER FORM

Any books from our AAT range can be ordered by telephoning 020-8740-2211. Alternatively, send this page to our address below, fax it to us on 020-8740-1184, or email us at **publishing@bpp.com.** Or look us up on our website: www.bpp.com

We aim to deliver to all UK addresses inside 5 working days; a signature will be required. Order to all EU addresses should be delivered within 6 working days. All other orders to overseas addresses should be delivered within 8 working days.

To: BPP Publishing Ltd, Aldine House, Aldine Place, London W12 8AW

Tel: 020-8740 2211   **Fax: 020-8740 1184**   **Email: publishing@bpp.com**

Mr / Ms (full name): _____

Daytime delivery address: _____

_____

Postcode: _____   Daytime Tel: _____

Please send me the following quantities of books.

	5/00 Interactive Text	8/00 DA Kit	8/00 CA Kit
FOUNDATION			
Unit 1 Recording Income and Receipts (7/00 Text)	☐	☐	
Unit 2 Making and Recording Payments (7/00 Text)	☐	☐	
Unit 3 Ledger Balances and Initial Trial Balance (7/00 Text)	☐	☐	
Unit 4 Supplying information for Management Control (6/00 Text)	☐	☐	
Unit 20 Working with Information Technology (8/00 Text)	☐		
Unit 22/23 Achieving Personal Effectiveness (7/00 Text)	☐		
INTERMEDIATE			
Unit 5 Financial Records and Accounts	☐	☐	
Unit 6 Cost Information	☐	☐	
Unit 7 Reports and Returns	☐	☐	
Unit 21 Using Information Technology	☐		
Unit 22: see below			
TECHNICIAN			
Unit 8/9 Core Managing Costs and Allocating Resources	☐		☐
Unit 10 Core Managing Accounting Systems	☐	☐	
Unit 11 Option Financial Statements (Accounting Practice)	☐		☐
Unit 12 Option Financial Statements (Central Government)	☐		
Unit 15 Option Cash Management and Credit Control	☐	☐	
Unit 16 Option Evaluating Activities	☐	☐	
Unit 17 Option Implementing Auditing Procedures	☐	☐	
Unit 18 Option Business Tax FA00(8/00 Text)	☐		
Unit 19 Option Personal Tax FA00(8/00 Text)	☐		
TECHNICIAN 1999			
Unit 17 Option Business Tax Computations FA99 (8/99 Text & Kit)	☐	☐	
Unit 18 Option Personal Tax Computations FA99 (8/99 Text & Kit)	☐	☐	

TOTAL BOOKS ☐ + ☐ + ☐ = ☐

@ £9.95 each = £ ☐

Postage and packaging:
UK: £2.00 for each book to maximum of £10
Europe (inc ROI and Channel Islands): £4.00 for first book, £2.00 for each extra
Rest of the World: £20.00 for first book, £10 for each extra

P & P   £ ☐

Unit 22 Maintaining a Healthy Workplace Interactive Text (postage free) ☐ @ £3.95   £ ☐

GRAND TOTAL £ ☐

I enclose a cheque for £ _____ (cheques to BPP Publishing Ltd) or charge to **Mastercard/Visa/Switch**

Card number ☐☐☐☐☐☐☐☐☐☐☐☐☐☐☐☐☐☐☐☐

Start date _____ Expiry date _____ Issue no. (Switch only)___

Signature _____

REVIEW FORM & FREE PRIZE DRAW

All original review forms from the entire BPP range, completed with genuine comments, will be entered into one of two draws on 31 January 2001 and 31 July 2001. The names on the first four forms picked out on each occasion will be sent a cheque for £50.

Name: _____   Address: _____

_____

_____

How have you used this Devolved Assessment Kit?
(Tick one box only)

☐ Home study (book only)

☐ On a course: college _____

☐ With 'correspondence' package

☐ Other _____

Why did you decide to purchase this Devolved Assessment Kit? *(Tick one box only)*

☐ Have used BPP Texts in the past

☐ Recommendation by friend/colleague

☐ Recommendation by a lecturer at college

☐ Saw advertising

☐ Other _____

During the past six months do you recall seeing/receiving any of the following?
(Tick as many boxes as are relevant)

☐ Our advertisement in *Accounting Technician* magazine

☐ Our advertisement in *Pass*

☐ Our brochure with a letter through the post

Which (if any) aspects of our advertising do you find useful?
(Tick as many boxes as are relevant)

☐ Prices and publication dates of new editions

☐ Information on Kit content

☐ Facility to order books off-the-page

☐ None of the above

Have you used the companion Interactive Text for this subject?   ☐ Yes   ☐ No

Your ratings, comments and suggestions would be appreciated on the following areas

	Very useful	Useful	Not useful
Introductory section (How to use this Devolved Assessment Kit etc)	☐	☐	☐
Practice Devolved Assessments	☐	☐	☐
Trial Run Devolved Assessments	☐	☐	☐
Content of Answers	☐	☐	☐
Layout of pages	☐	☐	☐
Structure of book and ease of use	☐	☐	☐

	Excellent	Good	Adequate	Poor
Overall opinion of this Kit	☐	☐	☐	☐

Do you intend to continue using BPP Assessment Kits/Interactive Texts/? ☐ Yes   ☐ No

Please note any further comments and suggestions/errors on the reverse of this page.

Please return to: Nick Weller, BPP Publishing Ltd, FREEPOST, London, W12 8BR

REVIEW FORM & FREE PRIZE DRAW (continued)

Please note any further comments and suggestions/errors below

FREE PRIZE DRAW RULES

1   Closing date for 31 January 2001 draw is 31 December 2000. Closing date for 31 July 2001 draw is 30 June 2001.

2   Restricted to entries with UK and Eire addresses only. BPP employees, their families and business associates are excluded.

3   No purchase necessary. Entry forms are available upon request from BPP Publishing. No more than one entry per title, per person. Draw restricted to persons aged 16 and over.

4   Winners will be notified by post and receive their cheques not later than 6 weeks after the relevant draw date.

5   The decision of the promoter in all matters is final and binding. No correspondence will be entered into.